Perfect Phrases for Writing Grant Proposals

Perfect Phrases for Writing Grant Proposals

**Hundreds of Ready-to-Use Phrases to Present
Your Organization, Explain Your Cause,
and Get the Funding You Need**

Dr. Beverly Browning

New York   Chicago   San Francisco   Lisbon
London   Madrid   Mexico City   Milan   New Delhi
San Juan   Seoul   Singapore   Sydney   Toronto

This is a *CWL Publishing Enterprises Book* produced for McGraw-Hill by CWL Publishing Enterprises, Inc., Madison, Wisconsin, www.cwlpub.com.

This publication is designed to provide accurate and authoritative information in regard to the subject matter covered. It is sold with the understanding that neither the author nor the publisher is engaged in rendering legal, accounting, or other professional services. If legal advice or other expert assistance is required, the services of a competent professional person should be sought.

> —From a Declaration of Principles jointly adopted by a Committee
> of the American Bar Association and a Committee of Publishers

McGraw-Hill books are available at special quantity discounts to use as premiums and sales promotions, or for use in corporate training programs. For more information, please write to the Director of Special Sales, Professional Publishing, McGraw-Hill, Two Penn Plaza, New York, NY 10121-2298. Or contact your local bookstore.

Contents

Contents

Contents

Contents

Part Three. Perfect Phrases for the Attachment Documents   179

Contents

Preface

Welcome to *Perfect Phrases for Writing Grant Proposals*! I know you're going to use this new and exciting book as a daily desktop reference when you're writing your grant proposals. From across the country, people have called and written to me indicating the need to have a list of my "words that work" in winning grant proposals. This book is the answer to hundreds—no, thousands of inquiries from new and veteran grant writers, nonprofit personnel, and many others who face the daunting task of trying to formulate the "perfect" phrases.

This book is for you! Calling all nonprofit executive directors or other staff searching for the right words! Calling all development directors who must also write grant proposals! Calling all designated grant or proposal writers and specialists who must work 24/7 to create the buzz words needed to win an infinity of grant awards! From the novice to the very experienced, this is your book!

When you're on deadline and need some great ideas for a winning Introduction and Background of Your Organization, turn to Part One, Chapters 1 through 5. You'll learn about Formats and how to write Introductions to the Applicant Organization, Current Programs and Activities, Target Populations, and Community Served and Partners.

Tired of your brain turning to gelatin when it's time to write the Description of Your Request? Turn to Part Two, Chapters 6 through 10, to learn about and how to write a compelling Need Statement, Purpose, Program Design, Management Plan, and Evaluation Plan.

Finally, Part Three, Perfect Phrases for the Attachment Documents is to help you finish off your grant proposal in grand style! Chapters 11 through 13 cover phrases and examples you can use for the Budget, Agency Structure, and Letters of Support section of your grant proposal.

Acknowledgments

When I was asked to write this book, I had the privilege of communicating with and getting to know John Woods at CWL Publishing Enterprises. It was through his patience and graciousness that I was able to see all of my *perfect phrases* come together in this adrenaline-filled book. Thanks, John, for thinking of me and opening the door to another major publishing corporation.

Next, I would like to tell the world about Margot Maley Hutchison, my literary agent at Waterside Productions, Inc. She has been by my side and leading me since my first major international publication. Margot, I am so very grateful for your professionalism, friendship, and faith. I contacted you about this book offer when your life was on a roller coaster of emotions due to your oldest son's diagnosis and ongoing treatment. Through your Web site, *www.teamsam.com*, I have come to know and love Sam.

Preface

I would like to give the highest acknowledgment to Sam Hutchison, "a loving, soccer-playing, heelie-wearing, taco-eating, video game-playing, bike-riding, Magic Treehouse book-reading, bionicle-building, transformer-transforming, brother-tormenting, brother-loving, baby brother-kissing, speed-loving six-year-old." Hats off to you, Sam!

Finally, I'd like to thank my husband, John, who has survived the writing of this 25th book and who keeps me going when my internal battery runs low. I love this husband of nearly 41 years and I want to declare this to my readers, here and now!

When all else fails, write. It is both therapeutic and productive ... Bev

Perfect Phrases for Writing Grant Proposals

Part One

Perfect Phrases for the Introduction and Background of Your Organization

Chapter 1
Typical Formats:
Writing What Funders Want to Read

This first chapter is organized to orient you to the types of writing formats you'll likely encounter when you start to research grantmakers and discover how they want you to *order* the information they ask for in your funding requests. Over the years (23 to be exact) that I've been writing grant proposals, I've discovered that all grantmaking organizations ask for the same type of information—some less, some more. While this book cannot possibly cover the dozens of request formats in use at any given time, I do want to give you the most commonly used writing formats. The most commonly requested formats are:

- *letter proposals* (also called *corporate letters*)
- *common grant applications*
- *government grant applications*
- *concept papers*

Once you know how to meet the funder's writing format, you can request funding support for just about everything your organization needs to serve its clients.

Grant proposals may be either solicited or unsolicited.

- **Solicited proposal**—The funding source (foundation, corporation, or government agency) issues a public announcement, often called an RFP (request for proposals), asking for written grant proposals for a funding priority established by its governing body.
- **Unsolicited proposal**—The applicant organization researches funding sources and submits written grant proposals to those whose past or current funding areas match the organization's proposal idea.

Many corporate and foundation funders have developed customized applications that they require you to fill out and submit. Since there are thousands of corporate and foundation funders with specific grant writing formats and applications (some are even online applications), Parts One and Two focus on the commonly used grant proposal formats. Even if you are faced with filling out a customized grant application for a funder, you should be able to transfer over everything you learn in this book to its narrative sections and attachments.

The letter proposal, common grant application, government grant application, and concept paper formats in this chapter share common narrative sections and "copy and paste" information. If you choose to use the letter proposal format, your request will be short and to the point. The common grant application format allows for more details and can even include some visual enhancements such as bolding, underlining, and italicizing. The government grant application proposal format is more comprehensive and lengthier, to provide grant application peer reviewers with key information needed to make a decision to fund or reject your proposal. Finally, the concept paper format is a cross between a letter proposal and a common grant application. Don't worry: I'll show you the main narrative sections for each of these formats.

The perfect phrases in the following chapters are meant to capture the attention of reviewers skimming your proposal's narrative sections and attachments and cause them to want to read more about your proposed project. In each chapter, you'll find phrases and words that leap off the page. When you incorporate these perfect phrases into your own grant proposals, you'll find that winning a grant award is not an impossible dream.

Letter Proposal or Corporate Letter Format (Narrative, Three to Five Pages)

The letter proposal is an abbreviated version of the common grant application format. *It's my favorite funding request format! I've used this format to win grant awards ranging in size from $5,000 to $250,000 for nonprofit organizations.* Small foundations and corporations prefer to receive funding requests in this form. But always call or e-mail a funder before submitting a proposal to inquire about the format they will accept.

If it's a letter proposal, it should be less than five typewritten pages and can be as few as three pages. A letter is just long enough to include the specifics about your program and not so long that the reader will lose interest and put it down—delaying a funding decision.

1. Amplify Needs. Write three opening sentences (use bullets for visual appeal) that capture the dire state of the need or problem. For example: "There are 4,000 homeless teenagers living on the streets of metropolitan Phoenix—90% survive dangerous elements, people, and weather; 10% are given pauper's funerals when no family members claim their remains." Use phrases that reek of gloom, doom, drama, and trauma!

2. Current Problem. Present the problem and include information about individuals and communities affected by the gap in services. If your organization needs staff training or something else that appears unrelated to providing services, still focus on the problems of your clients or constituents. You want the funder to feel the urgency of your grant proposal request by talking about how bad things are and how the cost to fix the problem will be far greater down the road if the problem is not addressed soon. Use phrases that contain lots of statistics and sources. (Footnote all statistics.)

3. Purpose Statement. Be direct and tell the funder why you're writing this proposal. Talk about the purpose of the funding, what their money will provide or create or expand, and how many members of your target population will be impacted. For example: "The purpose of this request is to expand street outreach interventions to *500* homeless teenagers in Phoenix, Arizona." Use phrases for your purpose that help you tell it and sell it.

4. Goals. Set goals for intervention or prevention (solving the problem) that are full of hope, promise, and future client results. For example: "The goal of our project is to provide homeless teenagers with temporary shelter and comprehensive psychosocial counseling to circumvent chronic long-term homelessness." Goals are not meant to be measurable—goals are reached because of measurable objectives or benchmarks that lead to their achievement. When you are writing goal statements, use phrases that reflect dreams.

5. Objectives. Set *s*pecific, *m*easurable, *a*ttainable, *r*ealistic, and *t*ime-bound (SMART) objectives or benchmarks. Every goal must have its own specific objectives or steps written in measurable terms. For example: "Decrease the current number of homeless teenagers living on the streets of Phoenix by 25% or more during the three-year project period by providing 120-day temporary shelter and 80 hours of comprehensive intervention counseling." Objectives must include the percentage of the proposed change, who's being targeted, and how and when the change will occur. Use phrases that shout accountability. Think benchmarks or quantifiable steps when writing these SMART phrases!

6. Project Timeline. Align your project timeline with the funder's award timeframe and your own implementation timetable. For example: "Project Start Date–June 1, 2007. Project End Date–May 31, 2008." You can adjust your project start and end dates to align with the actual grant award date. Use a phrase that is short and to the point. Remember: your timeline should begin as soon as the funding will be made available by the funder. Call to ask if you can't find any project start dates in the published information.

7. Grant Applicant. Introduce your organization to the funder; no one sends a check to an unknown recipient. Give a visual trip through your front door and focus on the operational details. For example: "The Northern Lights Homeless Shelter, founded in 1995, is located in Phoenix (Maricopa County), Arizona. With 27 full-time staff and 100 volunteers, the shelter provides temporary living accommodations for 500 homeless teenagers annually." Remember: don't ramble here. Use phrases that create a lasting memory for the grant reader.

8. Community Partners. List your community partners and talk about their roles in helping your organization further its purpose and its programs. Without partners, your proposal doesn't stand a chance of being funded. For example: "Goodwill Industries of Maricopa County has been a partner for 10 years. They are able to provide vocational training and job-related counseling to older teens who are emancipated from their parents and able to live independently." Use phrases that propel your partnership network's magnitude and strength.

9. Project Staff. Provide the qualifications of the personnel selected for the proposed project. Funders want to know you've selected the most capable people to administer and carry out the project's activities. Choose people who have related experience. For example: "Jill Jefferson will act as the Project Director. She has worked with homeless individuals for more than 20 years. Dr. Jefferson has a graduate degree in psychology from Columbia University Medical School and was the founder of the New York City Homeless Outreach Program." Use phrases that convey capability.

10. Evaluation. Include plans for monitoring the progress toward measurable objectives and reporting data findings to stakeholders. Also include details about who will conduct the evaluation, what type of data will be collected, how it will be collected, and the frequency of the data collection and reporting to stakeholders. The key terms to talk about in the Evaluation Plan are qualitative data and measurements and quantitative data and measurements. For example: "The evaluation plan includes developing data collection tools, determining the data sample percentage, and collecting stakeholder feedback to monitor quarterly progress points and determine the need for implementation modifications. The Northern Lights Homeless Shelter will contract with Larry Davidson, Senior Consultant for Social Programs Evaluation, Inc., to oversee all phases of the program evaluation. Mr. Davidson will assist in creating surveys, observation logs, and service quality testing instruments for each level of stakeholders. After rigorous data analysis and interpretation, stakeholder reports will be prepared and disseminated to report qualitative and quantitative outcomes." Use phrases that contain all of the evaluation buzz words.

11. Existing Resources. Describe the financial and physical assets of your organization. Funders don't want to award grants to bare-bones operations. Most grant applicants already have a building where their operations are based, as well as office furniture and equipment. Think about your resources, make a list, and write about them in a short narrative paragraph. For example: "The Northern Lights Homeless Shelter owns a three-acre, six-building campus in Central Phoenix. A recent facilities inventory revealed that the buildings are valued at $2.5 million and the furnishings and equipment are valued at $200,000." Use phrases that show the strengths of your organization's current assets.

12. Invitation. Make the sales pitch to potential funders, inviting them to invest in your organization. Here's an award-winning invitation: "The Northern Lights Homeless Shelter urgently seeks your financial partnership in its proposed Street Outreach Program for Homeless Teens. Your approval of a $250,000 grant award will help our staff to save the lives of 500 fragile, discon-nected, and near-death teens." Use phrases that ask and push the point with dire language.

13. Closing and Signature. The closing *Sincerely* is really out-dated. I like to close with this phrase: *With Urgency.* Also, remem-ber to have your Executive Director or Board of Director's President sign the letter proposal. Use a closing phrase that con-veys the urgency of the funding request to embed your organi-zation's need for financial support—right down to the last line in this writing format.

14. Attachments. Attach the project budget, the organizational budget, proof of nonprofit status, a list of the Board of Directors, and letters of support from previous clients. Use attachments to support your entire request document—the letter proposal—and to demonstrate to funders that you have a solid organiza-tional structure and loads of supporters.

Winning Approach

Write each letter specific to the funder that will receive it. Don't try to use one generic letter format to approach multiple fun-ders. I want you to learn from my mistakes, OK?

Common Grant Application Format (Narrative, Five Pages)

Mid-size to large foundations and corporations with formal cor-porate giving programs (those with staff and application-writing guidelines) expect to receive a full grant proposal. Many will accept the frequently used, highly recognized common grant application format. To be sure, call or e-mail to ask about the proposal format they'll accept. The common grant application format allows grantseekers to provide just enough information about their organization, its abilities, constituents served and their needs, and the proposed solution. Of course, a full project budget is required to complete the request.

1. Cover Form. This information fits on one page.
   a. Organization Name
   b. Tax-Exempt Status
   c. Year Organized or Founded
   d. Address
   e. Telephone Number
   f. Fax Number
   g. Director
   h. Contact Person and Title (if not the director)
   i. Grant Request Amount
   j. Period Grant Will Cover
   k. Type of Request
   l. Total Project Budget (if request is other than general operating support)
   m. Total Organizational Budget
   n. Starting Date of Fiscal Year
   o. Summary of the Organization's Mission
   p. Summary of Project or Grant Request

2. History and Accomplishments. Briefly describe your organization's history and major accomplishments. Talk about when it was founded, what it has done, and some notable accomplishments to date. The funder will want to see information on how many people were served and in what types of programs. Also, the funder will want to know if the organization received any awards or honorable mentions from community groups or government agencies. Use phrases that show longevity, experience, and community connectivity.

3. Current Operations. Describe your organization's current programs and activities. However, stay on track and talk about what is relevant to the grant proposal funding topic. Use phrases that highlight your premier programs and activities that shout your organization's ability to touch many types of audiences.

4. Constituency and Involvement. Include the people you are proposing to serve in all phases of your organization's planning, grant writing, and evaluation processes. Then write about their involvement in the proposal. Once funded, you may be asked to provide proof of past client or constituency involvement, so you should keep records of all client involvement, including meeting agendas with dates and topics discussed. Use phrases that demonstrate the input of many end recipients—all ages, equal gender representation, all ethnicities, and all socioeconomic levels.

5. Community and Partners. Inform the funder about the community where the proposed program will be implemented. The funder will be interested in the setting of the problem, socioeconomic trends, and community risk factors related to the target population. The funder also will want to read about your community partners—local businesses, government agencies, other nonprofits, and faith-based groups. Don't leave them guessing; list your partners and their roles in a two-column table to draw attention to agency names and resources available to your proposed program. Use phrases that show how each type of partner group supports your organization's ongoing efforts in its grant-funded programs.

6. Problem Statement. Present a realistic and accurate picture of the problem. Your writing must speak to the grant reader in terms of the severity of the problem, whether it's chronic or new, and who else is addressing the problem and why their approaches or resources are insufficient to eliminate or solve the problem. This section is heavily supported by current research on the problem in your community obtained from a comprehensive needs assessment. Use phrases that hit the grant reader at every level of his or her value systems.

7. Purpose and Description. Begin this section with a purpose of funding statement and a one-sentence description of the proposed solution. Everything you wrote about in the problem statement must be solvable in your program design. The assumption in grant writing is that all problems presented can be solved with financial input. Use phrases that are to the point and do not leave the grant reader guessing what it is you are planning to do with the grant monies.

8. Goals. Write futuristic goals that speak to a positive end for all targeted populations benefiting from the grant funding. Think future and think success. Here, you'll want to make sure your goals close the gaps identified in the problem statement. Use phrases that are consistent with what the funder prioritizes in its published list of areas of grants.

9. Objectives. Chart the steps your participants will take to reach the goals. Funders want to see accountability built into your objectives in terms of measurable or percentage-driven objectives. Write objectives with terms of decreases or increases. Use phrases that show manageable progressive steps toward the end of the grant funding timeframe.

10. Strategies. Outline which intervention or prevention models you'll use to pursue the goals and objectives. For example, if your organization has adopted a psychosocial counseling model that includes small support groups with role-plays or one with situational problem solving, you'll describe it here. This also is the section to write about best practices research and how it will be implemented with your proposal's target population. Use phrases that reflect your diligent Internet research findings and validate them with footnotes or endnotes.

11. Timelines. Write about the activities or tasks that will be necessary in order to implement the proposed strategies, achieve the objectives, and reach the goals. Funders expect to see reasonable timelines, so create a chart with the year divided into quarters, not months. Monthly timelines tend to cause stress and do not allow for implementation delays. Use phrases that show chronological activities or tasks that you plan to undertake.

12. Benefits. State who is going to benefit most from the grant award and how they will benefit. Think of benefits in terms of gained knowledge, changed behaviors, long-term self-sufficiency, and similar outcomes. Use phrases that demonstrate that your proposed grant-funded program will take participants or end recipients to a better place than where they would be without your interventions.

13. Key Personnel. Tell the funder who will be in charge of the program and if they have the education and experience to carry it out. Funders also look for personnel characteristics that align with the target population. For example, if your target population is homeless teenagers, you'll want to include some graduate-school social work interns in your key personnel. Why? These college-age students will likely have some recent teen parenting or teenage experiences themselves that will help them identify with the issues of being homeless teenagers. Use phrases that convey that only the best of the best will be hired or assigned to carry out the program's tasks.

14. Evaluation. Include a plan for evaluating the program's success on every level: target population members, staff, partners, information and referral agencies, volunteers, and anyone else impacted by the grant-funded program. Writing about your evaluation plan forces you to list all of your stakeholders and the type of feedback they can provide. Use phrases that shout accountability at all levels of knowing if and when you reach your measurable objectives.

15. Budget Narrative. Provide a detailed paragraph to explain and justify each line item in your proposal budget summary (line items and totals). You must remember that a funder can't read your mind. You'll need to break down to the last detail every line item included in your budget summary. For example: "In-State Travel—$815.60. This line item includes one trip to the state capital for three days of technical assistance training in the new homeless client-tracking software. Jason Everhart, Program Management Information Specialist, will attend this training. The training registration fee is $295. Lodging for Mr. Everhart at a nearby motel is $100 per night x 3 nights ($300). Meals are reimbursed at a rate of $40 per diem x 3 ($120). Mileage reimbursement is $.42 per mile x 240 miles round-trip for a total of $100.60. Total travel expenses: $815.60." Use phrases that present an accurate picture of the expenses, their cost, and your justification for including this in the proposed grant-funded budget.

16. Board of Directors. Give funders the added confidence that you have an experienced Board of Directors by including for each member name, contact information, position in the community, gender, ethnicity, and any other demographic that demonstrates connectivity between your Board members and the clients you're proposing to serve in your grant proposal. Use phrases that show the strong link between the Board's management ability and the program's administrative and direct services staffing structure.

17. Support. Attach letters of support from your partners and clients that are project-specific, talk about your organization's capacity to manage a grant-funded program, and indicate the type and value of support that will be provided. Generic letters aren't convincing, so it's important to have the people writing the letters use varied perfect phrases to produce credible support letters. Encourage them to use phrases that reflect the purpose of the grant funding request.

Winning Approach

Always call the funding source first to see if there are any specific attachments they want to see from first-time grant applicants.

Government Grant Application Narrative Format

Each government grantmaking agency has its own specific grant proposal forms and narrative writing format. The length of each narrative section also differs. However, they have some mandatory basics in common. Remember: always read the funder's specific guidelines and then write to the guidelines—to the letter.

1. Summary. Outline your proposed program to the grant peer reviewers (individuals selected to read and score government grant proposals). If you write the summary after you've written the entire grant proposal, you can copy and paste key sentences from the narrative to create it. The summary is limited to one page, no more. You'll need a sentence or two each about the need, the purpose of the program, the goals, the objectives, the evaluation plan, and the participant outcomes. Use short and concise phrases that present the entire picture of the application.

2. Introduction. Present information about your organization's mission, goals, and track record with other grantors. Peer reviewers also want to read about your organization's past and present operations that are related to the government grant funding area or priority. Use phrases that convince peer reviewers that your organization is *not* the new kid on the block!

3. Problem Statement. Write about the purpose for developing the grant proposal and the beneficiaries of the proposed program, including who they are and how they'll benefit. The problem must be presented in depth; cite supporting research—not older than five years. This validation process shows peer reviewers that your organization knows the problem exists and what other agencies are doing about it. You'll also write about alternative funding for solving the problem if there are not enough government grant funds to solve it. Use phrases that reflect research-supported data findings and that are relevant to the purpose of the government grant funding initiative.

4. Goals, Objectives, and Outcomes. Be conservative in what you promise when you write your measurable objectives and develop implementation timeframes. All types of funders expect you to write global goals, measurable objectives, and realistic outcomes for your target population. However, only government grantmaking agencies will take your measurable objectives and include them in the written grant agreement between the agency and your organization. Your promises could come back to haunt you financially. If your organization isn't achieving objectives in the promised timeframes, it could affect the next funding transfer. (Government grants are not awarded in total upfront; funds are released on a quarterly projection basis.) The perfect phrase I use most frequently in measurable objectives is "or more." I tend to lower the percentages I use in objectives and then add "or more" after the percentage. It's safe and allows room for progress failures. Use phrases that present a logical and realistic picture of how your plan for achieving success is solid and manageable during the length of the grant funding timeframe.

5. Methods and Design. Provide information about the activities and resources your organization has in terms of staff and partners to operate the project. These are also called *inputs*. Some government agencies will ask for the inputs to be presented in a Logic Model. For the model, you'll create a narrative or a table to pull out and highlight inputs, outputs, and short-term, intermediate, and long-term outcomes. You incorporate the Logic Model language to show connectivity between your identified resources (money, staff, volunteers, facilities, materials, and equipment), your proposed activities (outputs), and the outcomes (measurable objectives broken down into short-term, mid-term, and end-of-program progressive steps). If you write "Reduce chronic unemployment among homeless individuals by 30% or more by the end of Year 1" as a global objective, your short-term objective might be 10% by the end of the second quarter, your mid-term objective might be

30% by the end of the third quarter, and your long-term objective might be 30% by the end of the fourth quarter. Use abbreviated phrases that tell the story in realistic bullets and can convey the big picture to grant reviewers.

6. Evaluation. Write about doing a *product* evaluation and a *process* evaluation. Product evaluations assess the results of the project. Process evaluations examine how the project was conducted in terms of following the methods and design in the grant proposal and the effectiveness of the plan in meeting the goals and objectives. Your writing must convince grant peer reviewers that your organization understands the evaluation process and that you'll employ objective methods to determine the impact of the grant-funded program on your target population. Use phrases that demonstrate your knowledge of the evaluation process—even if you're new and unsure of how to proceed—and phrases that draw from the government agency's past evaluations of similarly funded national or regional programs.

7. Budget. Create a budget showing your organization's soft and hard cash match monies, your partners' soft and hard cash matches, and how government grant funds will take your proposed project to the finish line. When you create your project budget, make sure to write sufficient explanations in the budget detail narrative to support every dollar, requested and matching. Also carefully read the government grantmaking agency's instructions about rounding each line item either up or down to the nearest whole dollar. Failing to do this could cause your application to be rejected for funding consideration. Use phrases that echo the program design so that grant reviewers can connect what you've proposed to implement with the budget line items for the costs of implementation.

Winning Approach

Consider signing up to be a grant reader or peer reviewer for a government grantmaking agency. I've been participating in government grant application peer reviews for over a decade and just knowing how grant applications are scored (on a 1-to-100-point scale) and recommended for funding has helped me to improve my own funding success rate.

Concept Paper Format

It has become commonplace for some government grantmaking agencies to request a concept paper instead of a full-blown grant application. A complete grant application requires forms, a narrative, and lots of mandatory attachments. A concept paper, on the other hand, is easier to research and assemble and does not take as long to develop the writing format.

Here's the format that I use for concept papers when the grantmaking agency has no specific writing format guidelines.

1. Cover Sheet (one page). Create a cover sheet with the title of your proposed project and your contact information. State the name of the government funding agency you are writing the concept paper for and the name or identification number of the specific funding program. Include the length of the proposed project and your intended start date. Type this on your organization's letterhead stationery and have an authorized administrator sign off at the bottom. Make sure to add a date behind the signature and type the name of the individual signing the cover sheet. Use phrases that complete each information field succinctly.

2. Project Narrative (three to five pages). Write about why the project is needed and who will likely benefit. Include why these needs are not being met by other service providers. Tell the grant reader what your organization will do if funded and how and where you'll conduct project activities. Also, write about your evaluation process, if funded. Remember to conclude with how you'll get the word out about your project to potential participants, partners, and other interested parties. Use phrases that invite the grant reader to invite your organization to submit a full proposal.

3. Project Budget (**one page**). Create a budget summary (line items and amounts); show your cash or in-kind match for each line item. Use abbreviated phrases that demonstrate your ability to be financially prudent and understand cost-effective practices.

Winning Approach

Keep this paper short and to the point. Don't ramble or offer more information than the funder requests. Sometimes when funders request concept papers, they are testing your ability to follow instructions. Show them that you can!

Chapter 2
Experience and Achievement:
Impressing with Your History and Accomplishments

A s a grant proposal reviewer, I read many requests for funding that fail to provide sufficient information on the grant applicant organization—legal name, tax-exempt status, location, year founded and by whom, mission, and accomplishments. It's important to provide funders with a written tour of your organization.

Since you are introducing your organization to them on paper or via electronic application, you must familiarize grant readers with the recipient of their money. After all, who wants to give money to a stranger or unknown group? You can guide the tour by writing perfect phrases about your organization's history and accomplishments. Your writing must virtually bring grant decision makers into your organization by telling them what they will experience during a site visit.

A winning grant proposal or fundraising request must first orient the grant reader or reviewer with the logistics and purpose of the applicant organization. The type of grant proposal format you're writing may restrict the length of the narrative section, so you'll want to use only phrases that tell the story of your organization's history, experience, and accomplishments.

Elements of a Winning Experience and Achievement Section:

1. Introduce Your Organization.
2. State Your Organization's Accomplishments.
3. Provide a Virtual Tour of Your Organization.

1. Introduce Your Organization

Whether the funder you're submitting your proposal to is located in your community, your state, or out of state, you must introduce your organization as if you're writing to a stranger. You should never assume the funding agency is familiar with your organization.

Here are the essential information points you'll want to cover when you introduce your organization.

Give its legal name, a hint of its purposes, your tax-exempt status, and geographic location.

- The Children's Gate, Inc., a shelter for homeless children, is a 501(c)(3) nonprofit corporation located in Yuma (Yuma County), Arizona.

- Jefferson County Hospital Foundation, a fundraising arm for the county's only publicly owned health care facility, is a 501(c)(3) nonprofit corporation located in Lilac, Missouri.

- The Flint Area Chamber of Commerce, a membership entity for business owners, is a 501(c)(6) nonprofit association located in Flint (Genesee County), Michigan.

- The Bristol-Warren Regional School District, a public (nonprofit in revenue structure by state legislative act) Pre-K through 12th grade educational entity, is located in Bristol (Bristol County), Rhode Island.

- Medical Research Associates, LLC, a privately held for-profit medical research corporation, is located in New York City, New York.

- The World Life Nature Center, a Wyoming-based nonprofit organization (holds an IRS-approved 501(c)(3) letter of nonprofit determination), is located in Jackson Hole (Teton County).

■ Amity State University (grant applicant), a state-supported, public institution with a separate fiscal agent (ASU Education Foundation), is located in Amity (Aroostook County), Maine.

Tell a little bit more about its geographic location (the beginning of the virtual tour). In this next group of phrases, you do not want to paint a "come here for your next vacation" picture. Instead, begin to introduce the "not so nice" aspects of your location.

■ Yuma is still one of Arizona's most productive agricultural regions. Its proximity to California, where the cost of living is high, home foreclosures are numerous, and the afford-able rent market is limited, and its position on international immigration pathways from Mexico to Arizona create a vortex drawing in homeless families who often abandon their children in our community. Because Yuma is located in the extreme southwest of Arizona, many of the city and county social and human services agencies also extend their programs and services to thousands of Californians each year.

■ Jefferson County is located in the Missouri Boot Heel Region along the Tennessee and Arkansas borders. While it's close to I-55, the county is rural, isolated, and void of any major employers or corporations. The area's economy has been flat since the closing of over 100 agribusiness farms in the late 1980s. Thousands of cars pass through Jefferson County as they take the back roads to larger, more populated areas; however, few stop for roadside essentials.

- Flint, Michigan, has barely survived a decade of economic decline, automotive plant closings, outward migration of tens of thousands of families, and public school closings. While Genesee County has experienced residential and commercial real estate development steadily since the 1990s, its nucleus, Flint, has been gasping for oxygen for a long time. From a state takeover of the City of Flint to the closure of dozens of businesses and one major corporation, the city has been on life support far too long.

- Bristol, Rhode Island, is best known for having the oldest Fourth of July celebration in the nation. Amidst its festival appearance lie myriad problems, including adult illiteracy, high juvenile crime rates, and uncontrollable truancy. While the state is known for its achievements in education (many world-class public and private colleges), this little pocket of complex demographics is as isolated as the peninsula it sits on.

- New York City is the economic center for the Eastern seaboard states. Yet, few publicly acknowledge the respiratory ailments, diagnosed and undiagnosed, that continue to reduce longevity and quality of life for the city's public service workers. Last year, the city paid nearly $90 billion in fines to the U.S. Environmental Protection Agency for its high number of excessive particulate days. Many frequent commuters into the city wore air filtering masks to avoid respiratory illnesses.

- Teton County covers nearly 2.7 million acres. Nearly 97% of the land is federally owned or state-managed. The remaining 3% is heavily populated with multi-million dollar condominiums, palatial estates, and resorts that cater to the rich and famous. Few outsiders are aware of the World Life Nature Center; however, they have heard of Yellowstone National Park and the National Elk Refuge. While Hollywood has spilled over into Jackson Hole and Teton County, there is another economic level of residents that few ever read or talk about—the working poor.

■ Amity has 200 year-round residents; 50 are University employees. During the school year, the town's population swells to 2,000 with the influx of University students. Located in the largest county in the state (Aroostook), on the Canadian border, Amity's claim to fame is its record winter snowfall and its 10 churches that represent the common and not-so-common religious denominations. Nearly 25% of the University's students and 10% of its faculty come from Canada. Amity has few stores, so monies earned in Amity and elsewhere are not being spent in Amity!

Note: In the beginning of this virtual tour, my first one or two sentences are about the area where the grant applicant is located. This continuing virtual tour also must give the grant reviewer an early glimpse of "What's wrong with this picture?"

Include the year founded and by whom. (It's OK to add a little trivia here!)

■ The Children's Gate was founded in 1986 by Maxine Jackson, a former State of Arizona social worker and a community advocate for homeless children. Ms. Jackson saw hundreds of children who fell through the social services gap monthly during her state employment. Her overwhelming feeling of helplessness led her to found the Children's Gate.

- The Jefferson County Hospital Foundation was formed in 1971 by the Friends of Jefferson County Hospital and approved by the County Board of Commissioners. The Foundation provides the needed support to the hospital so that no one is denied treatment or other medical services.

- The Flint Area Chamber of Commerce was founded in 1958 by a group of 12 local business owners. The current Executive Director is the grandson of one of the founders. This multi-generational link continues to attract new members and reassure old members.

- The Bristol-Warren Regional School District was established in 1924 by the Rhode Island Department of Education. The District services two small towns that have been at odds with each other for decades over small trivial issues. Because of this political divide, there are two governing boards that preside over the District.

- Medical Research Associates, LLC, was incorporated in 2002 by six medical specialists and four research scientists who had previously worked for the crude oil and tobacco industries. Feeling high levels of guilt over the research findings for their respective industries, these individuals met at a clean air conference, bonded quickly, and began to plan how to start and sustain their own research corporation.

- The World Life Nature Center was founded in 1982 by Robert Redford, who saw a need to develop an animal preserve on land that would have likely been overdeveloped for commercial purposes.

State the organization's mission. Keep the mission section brief. You'll want to save room for the next section.

- The Children's Gate mission is to provide a safe long-term residential shelter for homeless children who have been abandoned by their families.

- The Jefferson County Hospital Foundation's mission is to provide financial relief for the county's only health care facility so that it can continuously deliver critically needed health care services to the Missouri Boot Heel Region.

- The mission of the Bristol-Warren Regional School District is to provide high-quality education programs and services to the residents of Bristol County.

- The vision for Medical Research Associates, LLC, can be seen in its simple, yet effective mission statement: "Empower the minds of those with the research skills and answers to complex health issues so that they may experience infinite wisdom in developing new approaches to diagnosing and treating respiratory disease."

- The mission of the World Life Nature Center is to protect and preserve Wyoming's native wildlife species while promoting the importance of designating "no hunt, no kill" zones.

- Amity State University's mission and vision focus on providing the highest quality of postsecondary education services for its diverse customer base. This base includes students, faculty, administrators, support staff, and the greater community of Amity, Maine.

Note: I've used the same nonprofit and for-profit organizations for the first set of perfect phrases: Introduce Your Organization. Now, let's look at some new organizations for the next section.

2. State Your Organization's Accomplishments

Nothing says more about the worth of your organization than its strides in making a difference among its service population and the recognition it's received for its efforts. Recognition includes not only honors but also grant awards, which may be thought of as financial endorsements of an organization's work. Along with accomplishments, you'll want to mention grant awards your organization has received. Just make sure you list only the most noteworthy accomplishments and awards.

For social and human services organizations, emphasize the total number of clients served in the past fiscal year. Mention any special recognition and a few of your largest grant awards.

■ Last year, the Boys & Girls Club of Jones County provided academic and recreational programs for over 1,000 youth, ages 6 to 17 years old. In 2007, the Mary Davis McDonald Children's Trust Fund awarded the Club two grants, one for program development and the second for operating expenses. For the first time in 10 years, the Club had an operating budget of $500,000. This was due, in part, to receiving the interest earned on an endowment established by the Board of Directors in 2002. To date, the Directors' Endowment Fund, managed by the Jones County Community Foundation, has generated $100,000 annually in interest. The Club has been able to expand its programs and retain its dedicated staff.

■ Insight admitted 678 substance abuse clients last year. The organization was recognized by the U.S. Department of Health and Human Services Substance Abuse and Mental Health Services Administration as a model for treatment and aftercare programs. Insight is accredited by the State of Utah, the American Association of Counseling Professionals, and the Murtaugh County Substance Abuse Service Providers Authority. Most recently, the Salt Lake Human Services Coordinating Council recognized Insight for its excellence in client services.

If your organization is open to visitors (e.g., museums, art societies, symphonies, zoos, planetariums, and festival groups), write about the total number of visitors last year. Also, include any honors, recognitions, and special tributes.

■ The Cave Creek Zoological Society had 5,000 visitors last year. The Zoo was recognized for its native-like panda habitat by the U.S. Japan Animal Exchange Committee. May 24 of each year, the mayor of Cave Creek honors the Zoo by designating the entire day as "Let's Go to the Zoo Day." Our largest grant award, from the Joseph and Jackie Hardy Foundation, enabled the Society to build a $1 million reptile center. The Society is proud to state and advertise that the Zoo has had no visitor accidents or animal injuries or escapes—something many of our counterparts around the country cannot report.

■ Last year, the Merry Muppets String Quartet performed 26 times before a total of 5,400 people. Ticket sales were at an all-time high, which led the Idaho Council of the Arts to bestow an award to our Quartet for leading the state in audience expansion and diversity. Much to the Quartet's surprise, audience members come not only from the northern region of Idaho, but also from Montana and Washington. We've even had visitors from the Canadian provinces of Alberta and British Columbia.

For units of municipal or state government, write about your major public service accomplishments.

■ The City of Hot Springs recently completed its citizen satisfaction survey. Over 27,000 residents completed the five-page survey evaluating their satisfaction with city services and facilities. Approximately 79% of the respondents indicated high levels of satisfaction in the quality and quantity of city amenities. Last year, the City received over $6 million in community improvement grants to expand city parks and public transportation and to begin the first hub for a wireless city network. The voters overwhelmingly approved a bond issue for $8 million to build a new Civic Center complex (convention center, outdoor theater, and six-story five-star resort hotel).

■ The Wyoming Department of Labor oversees the state's 29 One-Stop Centers and provides pass-through funds to train and find employment for thousands of unemployed and underemployed Wyoming residents annually. Two years ago, the U.S. Department of Labor recognized Wyoming for its stellar employment and training programs. To date, the Wyoming Department of Labor has received over $20 million in federal grant awards. Although Wyoming has not been a hub for Fortune 500 corporations, it has been able to achieve consistently high job placement rates by using small to mid-size employer networks in each region.

For public school districts, charter schools, private schools, community colleges, vocational-technical centers, colleges, and universities, write about your academic accomplishments, including graduation rates, new program enrollments, and professional affiliation recognitions.

- The Buckeye Academy is Far West Valley's only charter school that has grown 50% annually in K–5 enrollments. While our school receives most of its funding from the state Department of Public Instruction, we were able to win over $250,000 in grant awards last year. These monies enabled the Academy to create an interpretive garden for visually impaired students. Community recognition for the garden was so great that the local garden society honored the Academy with its "Creative Project of the Year" award. Over the past two decades, graduates of Buckeye Academy have maintained their 4.0 (A) grade point averages throughout middle school, high school, and college. The Academy has a strong alumni network that holds an annual fundraiser that nets between $5,000 and $10,000 each year.

- Millstone State University is continually recognized for its high graduation rates. (For the past 20 years, 90 percent of students enrolling at one of our campuses have completed their studies and graduated on time.) The U.S. Department of Education recently awarded the University $1.5 million for an Upward Bound Program. Dedicated faculty members created a $50,000 Millstone Scholarship Fund in 2000 and have continued to garner community support, enabling the Fund to achieve a current balance of $552,000. To date, 10 worthy high school students have

received four-year fully paid scholarships to Millstone—
students who otherwise would not have been able to
afford the tuition on their own.

*For businesses (for-profit) and individual researchers or principal
investigators, write about your service, product, or research suc-
cesses, and any recognitions related to the grant project topic.*

- AmiCan, Inc. has been an industry leader for night vision
  equipment since its founding. The All Red Penetrating
  Night Goggles developed for the U.S. military in the early
  1970s are still in use today. Over 100,000 units have been
  shipped to military bases worldwide. One hundred percent of AmiCan's administrators recently completed ISO
  9000 quality management systems training. The U.S.
  Department of Homeland Security lists AmiCan's products
  in its Knowledge Resource Base inventory of approved
  first-responder equipment. This listing enables first respon-
  ders (firefighters and police) to apply for up to $5,000 in
  free equipment annually from the government.

- Dr. Eric Robertson is a nationally known genetic scientist.
  He has received numerous awards and recognitions for his
  ongoing work in human genome therapy. For the last five
  years, Dr. Robertson has been selected as the keynote
  speaker for the International Society of Biotechnology
  Researchers. Most recently, he received approval from the
  Federal Drug Administration to conduct research on new
  orphan drugs that can repair a diseased cell's membrane.
  This breakthrough initiative will propel Dr. Robertson to
  the top of his field and place him at the forefront for additional worldwide recognition.

3. Provide a Virtual Tour of Your Organization

Up to this point, you've given the grant reader the most important information about your organization, your business, or yourself, the grant applicant. Now it's time to take the reader on a virtual tour of your facilities.

- The Uptown Urban League is housed in a former strip mall on the east side of Milwaukee. The 20,000-square-foot facility houses administrative offices, a vocational training center, client counseling areas, a wireless conference facility, a clothing bank, a food distribution center, and a health care screening office. Our inner-city location enables clients with the most dire needs to access our services without transportation barriers.

- White Mountain Community College has a 40-acre campus in Show Low that sits amidst pristine 100-foot pine trees. The four buildings (academic classrooms, administration, applied laboratory programs, and maintenance) total 100,000 square feet. The winding driveway allows visitors to take in the beauty of the elevation and the rural countryside. The College's size makes it a gathering point for the entire community, including tribal nations that hold their annual powwow in nearby Pinetop and use the campus and its facilities for their welcome reception and meetings.

- The Martindale Public Library is a new 50,000-square-foot glass-and-steel facility. Community access accommodations include a moving sidewalk, 30 private study booths, wireless free Internet connectivity throughout the building, and a Coffee Meet and Greet outdoor café. The Children's Department was brightly painted by local artists who had a flair for neon colors. Children who use the library's services are taken on a memorable trip through story land, as each wall depicts a famous fairy tale.

■ The Commonwealth of Virginia's Department of Housing is located on G Street in downtown Norfolk. Accessible by public and private transportation, the Department prides itself on the new Public Information reception area. On entry, one will find racks of brochures answering every possible question about how to find, finance, and maintain all types of housing in Virginia. Multiple skylights provide natural lighting and invite the public to stroll through an indoor garden and visit an outdoor restaurant beside a waterfall.

How will you know how much to write? It's going to depend on the type of grant proposal or application you're writing and the funder's specific guidelines for page limits on sections or the complete narrative.

Perfect Phrases to Include in a Letter Proposal

■ Quick, short phrases turn a stranger into a funder. (Remember to incorporate a sentence or two from each of the three elements of a winning narrative section.)

Perfect Phrases to Include in a Common Grant Application

■ Two to three paragraphs of phrases to give the funder an inside look at who you are, where you are, what you do, who you do it for, how well you do it, and what your facility looks like.

Perfect Phrases to Include in a Government Grant Application

- Lengthy, detailed paragraphs of phrases to bring the grant reader virtually into your community and your organization.

Chapter 3
Programs and Activities:
Showing and Telling
What You Do Well

Organizational characteristics include the programs that you manage and the related activities that these programs provide to your target population or constituents. The older an organization, the more current programs and activities it will have to list in this section of the grant proposal narrative. The newer a program, the more you'll have to write creatively to bandstand its limited characteristics.

In this chapter, I've written perfect phrases for both well-established (decades old) and recently implemented types of programs and activities. A winning grant proposal or funding request must demonstrate to the investors (corporations, foundations, state and federal government grantmaking agencies) that the applicant organization knows how to plan, pilot, implement, and track the outcomes for both past and current programs. Without this "credentialing" information in the narrative, your potential investor has no assurance of your ability to manage the program you are proposing to fund with their monies.

Elements of a Winning Programs and Activities Section:

1. Present Relevant Current Programs.
2. Share the Outcomes of Relevant Past and Current Programs.
3. Show Funders Your Program Implementation Strengths.

1. Present Relevant Current Programs

It's important that you understand the grantmaker's definition of "relevant." If you are applying for grant funds to create a skate park in your community, then write about other community-wide programs and activities your organization has provided (sports, arts and culture, education, health, and so forth). However, if you're applying for grant funds to conduct HIV prevention education, then the current programs and activities that you write about must be relevant or related to this area. The grantmaker wants to know if your organization has experience with planning and delivering programs and activities to the same population you're proposing to serve. In other words, they don't want to read multiple paragraphs about your midnight basketball program for low-income youth residing in public housing. The basketball program is not significantly relevant to the HIV prevention education program you're proposing.

List your current programs and activities in chronological order, beginning with the most recently implemented programs.

■ The Orange County Tourist and Convention Bureau's programs include:
  1. Movies Now!—Started in 2000 after movie production companies relocated their sets to other counties and states. Movies Now! offers multiple amenities, which include shutting down freeways and major thoroughfares for filming purposes.
  2. International Visitors Marketing Program—Started in 1990 to attract families and business owners from other

countries to the county's many multi-use amenities. Marketing efforts target both developing and economically stable countries.

3. First Stop for Conventions Program—Started in 1985 to showcase the original Orange County Convention Center, which has since been remodeled and expanded to 900,000 square feet with six center stage auditoriums and 45 breakout rooms. Six restaurants offer conference participants multiple choices and prices.

■ The Copper State Zoo's current programs include:

1. Animals Here and Now Education Program—Started in 2005 to increase memberships among families with young children and senior citizens. Both individual and group tours are available to allow visitors "hands on" with all types of Zoo animals.

2. Community and Conservation Action Program—Started in 2000 to reintroduce retiring animals (too old for active zoo life) back into their natural habitat, including returning them to their native countries.

3. Unconditional Friends Program—Started in 1998 to encourage physically and mentally challenged people to visit the Zoo. Group home residents and individuals residing with their families pet and hold the more docile animals in the Friendship Garden.

■ The Metropolitan Transit Authority's (MTA) current programs include:

1. Able Ride Program—Started in 1995 to provide full access to individuals with disabilities. Eighty percent of the 400-bus fleet can accommodate disabled riders. In

2005, the Authority added 50 Ride on Demand (ROD) handicapped-accessible, nine-passenger mini-vans to its fleet.

2. MTA Museum—Founded in 1975 to capture changes and trends in mass transit vehicles, the museum has been a showpiece for regional and out-of-state visitors. To date, there are 100 different transportation vehicles housed in the museum. Six of the old buses have been converted into trendy food court restaurants with themes linked to the decades in which they were used.

■ The Cheyenne Public Schools' current programs include:

1. Tech/Prep Program (started in 1990)—Enables high school juniors and seniors to dually enroll in vocational skill building courses and college technical courses. Students earn credits at both institutions and when they graduate they are automatically accepted into Cheyenne Community College. In addition, the College provides partial and full scholarships to all students completing both levels of study with a grade point average of 3.5 or higher.

2. Migrant Education Program (started in 1985)—Provides mobile classrooms in rural areas for children ages 3 to 17 years old of transient farm workers. The program teaches core curriculum areas (mathematics, social studies, English language arts, and science) in a fast-track mode, covering one week of conventional classroom lessons in two days.

3. Early Childhood Program (started in 1980)—Targets children 3 to 5 years old and encompasses the whole

family to provide parenting education, developmental awareness, early health screenings, and adult literacy training.

- The ABC Day Care Center's current programs include:
  1. Infants R Us Care—Operating since 2005, this program allows parents of infants who are at least 6 weeks old but not yet beginning to walk to take advantage of high staff-infant ratios (1:3) in a highly supervised and monitored child care service.
  2. Terrific Toddlers—Operating since 2003, this program is designed for young children from the time they begin walking up to age 4. This day care program uses the state's early childhood curriculum and incorporates parent/child play time at the Center and at home. Small groups of parents meet at weekly, conveniently planned parent/child play sessions supervised by an early childhood development specialist and a parent educator.
  3. School Readiness—Operating since 2000, this program enrolls children who are age 4 in a fully certified, state-licensed preschool program to prepare them for kindergarten readiness assessments.

- Medical Staffing Services' current programs include:
  1. Physicians Now! (2004)—Locates and screens U.S.-licensed physicians to fill staffing shortages in medical clinics, urgent care centers, and hospital emergency rooms. Serves 10 northern California counties and has the capability of picking up staff via helicopter from convenient locations in their communities and deliver-

ing them to remote, mountainous areas for single- or multiple-shift assignments. Physicians are paid at the end of every day via automated payroll deposits. All lodging, ground travel, and meal expenses are covered by Medical Staffing Services.

2. Long-Term Teams (1994)—Places nursing assistants, practical and registered nurses, and physician's assistants in assignments of 30 days or longer. Some nursing homes and large medical facilities have contracted our personnel for as long as 12 months. Personnel signing a long-term team contract and reporting for work 90 scheduled days without an absence receive a $1,000 attendance bonus. This bonus is available every quarter to discourage call-ins and absences.

- The City of Holbrook Police Department's current programs include:

1. Neighborhood Crime Prevention Outreach (2006)— Every officer is assigned to the neighborhood in which he or she lives. When two or more officers live in the same neighborhood, assignments are made to nearby areas in need of an officer's ongoing presence. Officers plan and facilitate neighborhood crime prevention education meetings and socializing events for children and adults. This citizen-level personalization approach enables the officers to begin and maintain open communications with all residents.

2. Child Find (2000)—This program is operated from the Department's mobile command center, which travels throughout the city to fingerprint and take pictures of

children age 12 and younger. The prints and photos are then scanned into the Child Find database. When a child goes missing, the Department is able to issue local, regional, statewide, and national Child Find alerts to law enforcement officials.

3. Young Volunteer Police Cadets (1997)—This program encourages high school age youth to become volunteer police cadets. After completing a rigorous screening and training program (offered each summer for six weeks), youth are assigned to their neighborhood officer and can accompany them on patrol (back seat only and no access to firearms) and help with community programs and events. The youth are issued light blue uniforms clearly marked "City of Holbrook Police Cadet."

■ The Michigan Department of Labor and Economic Growth's current agencies and programs include:

1. Jobs, Education, and Training (JET)—Created at the beginning of 2005, this program funds expedited employment and training pilot programs across the state for members of underemployed and unemployed high-risk populations. Training and placement in non-traditional, high-demand occupations is supported for up to 18 months. JET is a new way of delivering employment support services to these populations. It breaks from the historical approach of training unskilled people and placing them in supported employment settings—all within a six-month timeframe—and expecting them to succeed with little, if any support mechanisms in place to foster employment skills building and job placement sustainability.

2. Wind and Solar Energy Initiative—Twenty years ago, the Legislature created incentives to encourage individuals and businesses to install alternative energy systems to preserve the state's traditional energy resources. Wind energy systems use the wind to generate electricity: the wind blows blades, which turn and spin the generator shaft. Solar energy systems capture sunlight and convert it into electricity.

■ Project Green Space's current programs include:

1. Research and Development—In 2002, our group contracted with scientists to begin a study of the relationship between green space and physical activities. It was our belief that in urban areas where green space is at a premium, fewer individuals partook in rigorous outdoor physical activities. The study has been ongoing and now enjoys the full support of the Ministry of Health.

2. The Pickering Lands Initiative—In 2000, the government determined that is was critical for the private sector to take the lead in preserving sensitive lands for future generations. The Pickering Lands Initiative is an effort to preserve 5,562 acres adjacent to federally owned areas.

2. Share the Outcomes of Relevant Past and Current Programs

When I write about the program outcomes, I like to use a **bold font** to emphasize outcome numbers. I also <u>underline key phrases</u> that I want to leap off the page and catch the reader's attention.

- Movies Now! has brought **$20 million** to the County's coffers since 2000. Over **300 movies** have been filmed on location. The County receives credits at the end of each film. Tourism has **increased by 50% annually** since 2001. Movies Now! has <u>enticed three studios to relocate to Orange County</u>, resulting in **145 new jobs** and future tax revenues **exceeding $5 million** over the next 10 years.

- The International Visitors Marketing Program has propelled Orange County to the forefront when it comes to world travelers. The Program's Web site receives **1,000 hits a day**, seven days a week. To date, over **5,000 families** have <u>contacted the Program for a list of tourism events, lodging accommodations, and nearby attractions</u>. In 2006, **40 new businesses** relocated from overseas to Orange County—15 of which are traded publicly on international markets.

- The First Stop for Conventions Program has attracted **30 national and international association conventions** annually, with an **average attendance of 2,000 or more**. In addition, convention exhibitors have paid **over $1 million annually** in staging fees to the contractors servicing deliveries, setups, food services, and outbound freight arrangements. <u>Unduplicated revenues</u> for the County have **exceeded $100 million** over the past decade.

- The Animals Here and Now Education Program has been solely responsible for attracting **12,000 school-age children** from the region's <u>435 public and private schools</u> who arrive via buses for group tours. Most notable is the <u>feedback from school teachers, administrators, and parents</u> who credit the program with helping especially shy children express their thoughts while at the Zoo and on return to the classroom. It seems they just can't contain the excitement!

- The Community and Conservation Action Program has <u>formed alliances with animal habitats in Central and South America</u>. To date over **100 retiring animals** have been returned to their natural habitats. Protected by well established non-governmental organizations that have created preserves, the animals are allowed to roam free safe from predators and free from daily visitors.

- In the Unconditional Friends Program, positive feedback has come from adult day care centers and senior citizens facilities that bus their residents in for the program. In 2006, nearly **1,000 individuals** with Alzheimer's disease were brought to the Zoo for therapeutic reasons. Feedback indicated that even with their disease-related memory loss, they were <u>able to relate petting some of our tamer animals to owning pets in the past—no matter how long ago they owned their pets</u>.

- The Able Ride Program has attracted nearly **10,000 riders**. Approximately **50% are quadriplegics** who require and receive full assistance. ROD service has **logged over 6,000 miles annually** in the metro area. Rider surveys show that <u>without Able Ride, many challenged individuals would not be able to leave their homes to work, shop, or enjoy the metro area's many amenities.</u>

- The MTA Museum has met and exceeded its annual projections for visitors for the past three years—topping attendance at **7,500 in 2006**. This high attendance shows increasing levels of public interest in mass transportation trends and vehicles. Some <u>families tour the museum at least once monthly</u>, bringing neighbors, extended family members, and out-of-town visitors. We don't know if it's the museum's transportation relics or the four-star restaurants in the international food court area! Calls to similar museums show that the MTA Museum is unique in generating more revenue from entry fees, which totaled **$375,000** last year.

- **Ninety percent of high school students** completing the Tech/Prep Program have also <u>completed their community college studies and earned associate degrees</u> along with one- or two-year occupational certificates.

- The mobile van logs **3,000 miles each summer** <u>delivering basic education skills</u> to nearly **1,000 migrant youth** living in rural farm settings with their parents and extended family members. Over **75% of migrant students** are able to complete **one entire grade level** for multiple core curricular areas in six weeks or less.

- Each year, the Early Childhood Program conducts an average of **500** <u>early health screenings</u>, **60** <u>parent education classes</u>, and **200** <u>hours of adult literacy sessions</u>.

- Although this is the Center's newest program, it is by far its most popular! The Center has maintained a waiting list of **over 50 children** whose families are eager to enroll them in Infants R Us Care. Licensed for **15 children**, the program has <u>operated at maximum capacity since its first week</u>. In its **two-year history**, there have been **no incident reports** or unhappy parents.

- Terrific Toddlers has served **200 children annually** (unduplicated counts) since its opening. **Ten percent** of our families have at least two children who qualify for Terrific Toddlers. Our long history of <u>making our services affordable</u> enables them to benefit from our <u>multiple-child discount</u>—**25% off individual child fees**.

- School Readiness is our premier program. Since 2000, the Center has **graduated 350 children** from this state-approved preschool program. **One hundred percent of children** <u>who have completed the School Readiness Program pass the state's Kindergarten Readiness Assessment</u>. **Eighty percent of the Center's staff** working in the School Readiness program are retired public school teachers.

- Physicians Now! has a pool of **135** general practitioners, **35** surgeons, **245** emergency medicine specialists, **10** internists, and 27 pediatricians. Approximately **25%** are <u>new physicians who have recently passed their medical board examinations</u>. **Fifty percent** have retired from their full-time practices and signed up because they were bored with their time unplanned and unscheduled. The others have part-time practices, for varying reasons, and want to diversify their experiences.

- The **600 health professionals** registered with Long-Term Teams represent **25%** of the available health care workforce in our county. In 2006, their assignments have resulted in **8,000** hours of service as they have filled in for vacationing or ill health care workers. Last winter, during the snow storm of the decade, <u>every worker in our database</u> was assigned to cover for personnel who could not report for work. **One hundred percent of the initial Long-Term Teams contracts** with health care providers are still intact after 13 years because of our ability to provide qualified and dedicated health professionals for indefinite assignments.

- The Neighborhood Crime Prevention Outreach Program has been responsible for reducing neighborhood crime by **75%** in one year. **Twenty** dedicated law enforcement officers delivered **80 educational workshops** in their assigned neighborhoods and found corporate sponsors for community picnics, sports events, and a city-wide festival. The festival was attended by **12,000** persons, <u>who were given pamphlets on crime prevention action steps</u>. Approxi-mately **35%** of persons attending the festival were from <u>outside the City of Holbrook</u>.

- Child Find has been responsible for issuing **1,750** national alerts for missing children. The local database has collected fingerprints and photographs for every child living in our town (**4,250 records**). In 2006, **six alerts** that were issued were for local children who were taken by a non-custodial parent. All six children <u>were returned home safely</u> after they were found in neighboring counties and states by law enforcement officers who had received the alert bulletin.

Programs and Activities

- Since its inception, the Young Volunteer Police Cadets program has graduated **156** high school students. Of this number, **65%** have graduated from high school and entered the local community college's associate degree program for law enforcement. Of the **27** current graduates, **100%** are employed by our Department. A survey of the students still working on their degrees shows that **90%** plan to work within 100 miles of our city.

- JET has helped **2,500** individuals successfully transition from welfare to work. Approximately **60%** of those entering employment are earning **$12 or more per hour**. The **40%** who have been earning less were also simultaneously enrolled in an occupational trade program to improve their employment skills. The most recent evaluation report indicates that these individuals are likely to earn **$18 or more** per hour after graduation and trade certification.

- Over the last two decades, **135** mid-size to large (500 or more employees) manufacturing plants have installed wind or solar energy systems. **Ten percent** of the state's households have installed either solar or wind systems. These energy-saving applications have reduced electricity bills for businesses and families by **more than $1 million**.

- Research studies published by Project Green Space have been presented to over **50** foreign ministries at world conferences and United Nations hearings on world environments. Studies show that when green spaces are created in major urban areas (500,000 persons or more) **40% of residents** will walk, run, or participate in high-endurance sports **two or more times per week**.

- To date the Pickering Lands Initiative has received financial support to preserve **50%** of its <u>total land preservation goal of 5,562 acres</u>. The Initiative has attracted the attention of **12 provincial environmental groups** that actively hold annual fundraisers and **donate 100%** of their proceeds to Project Green Space.

3. Show Funders Your Program Implementation Strengths

Before you end the Programs and Activities section of your grant proposal, it's important to write a sentence or two about your organization's program implementation strengths. Grantmakers need to know that if they give you a 12-month grant award you won't still be wondering halfway through the funding cycle how to get the program started. Regardless of the red tape in your organization that may slow program start-up, you must make an earnest effort to show that you have outstanding program implementation strengths. *Be brief—but make a lasting impression that you're the right organization for the grant!*

- Orange County Tourist and Convention Bureau has been implementing programs that have resulted in measurable outcomes for decades. Our procurement policies enable us to quickly subcontract with small businesses that can provide start-up implementation services within 72 hours of receiving a funding award.

- The Copper State Zoo's Board of Directors supports the Zoo's administration and meets as often as needed to approve incoming grant funds so that programs can begin hiring and training within 30 days of receiving notification of funding.

- The Metropolitan Transit Authority operates under site-based financial practices, enabling it to make quick decisions internally without having to seek Commission approval. The Authority has created multiple programs and successfully integrated them into the regional strategic transportation plan without objection or delay.

■ The Cheyenne Public Schools are able to quickly jumpstart grant-funded programs. The Board of Education has created a policy labeled "Start Now." Our schools are able to quickly hire and train workers and start projects within 45 days of funding notification.

■ The ABC Day Care Center is managed by a team of three persons. They make decisions quickly and implement programs under the scrutiny of staff, parents, and the state Department of Education. To delay or err is not an option in our quality-driven environment.

■ Medical Staffing Services is able to quickly approve receipt of grant funds and begin new program start-up tasks. Of the 13 previously funded grant programs, 100% have been up and running within 14 days of receipt of funds.

■ The City of Holbrook Police Department is one of six agencies in the City of Holbrook's governmental structure. The Department must receive permission (in the form of a resolution) from the Council before it can accept any grant awards or begin expenditures related to program implementation. This process takes 45 days and cannot be shortened. However, the Council will certify that the grant-funding activities will begin no later than 60 days after the notification of a grant award to the Department.

■ The Michigan Department of Labor and Economic Growth is a state agency. Its programs are implemented as fast as governmental processes allow and there is rigorous public scrutiny on all new programs. Accountability and effectiveness are the two highest indicators for all of the agency's programs—funded both by the private and public sectors.

- Project Green Space has not been able to move as quickly as it initially planned because of numerous demonstrations and public meetings. However, it is noteworthy that thousands of acres have been purchased from private landowners and potentially threatening commercial investors. Our past progress in land acquisition reveals a slow, but steady pace in preserving sensitive lands.

How do you know how much to write? Remember: the length of your response is determined by the grant-maker's application format guidelines.

Chapter 4
Target Population:
Talking About Working with
Your Target Population

When grantmaking agencies ask you to describe your target population, they expect you to tell them, in great detail, about the people you currently serve and/or those you plan to serve in the grant-funded program. You can't just write about the target population in generalities. Writing this high-point peer review section of the grant proposal narrative requires that you first research past and current demographics on the groups or subgroups first.

Some reliable places to find target population demographics include the county economic development agency, county or state health departments, the Annie E. Casey Foundation's Kids Count Web site (www.kidscount.org), and the U.S. Census Bureau's State and County Quick Facts Web site (quickfacts. census.gov). If your organization or another in your community or state has conducted a recent (no more than three years old) community needs assessment, you can also find great demographics in that report. Search for everything you need on the Internet—it's quick and you can cite each source in a footnote. I usually cite all demographics using this format: *In 2004, the Moose County Health Department issued a Risk Factor report showing that teenage pregnancies had increased by 14% over the 2000 levels countywide.*[1]

Elements of a Winning Target Population Section:

1. Provide Current Demographics for the Target Population You Already Serve.
2. Demonstrate Their Roles as Stakeholders in Your Proposed Program.
3. Show Funders How Target Population Input Impacts Strategic Planning.

1. www.moosecounty.gov/health_department_reports.html. Retrieved online March 2, 2007.

1. Provide Current Demographics for the Target Population You Already Serve

Grantmakers want to read recent information about your target population. Don't cite statistics over five years old unless you're doing a comparison between your most current statistics and monumental milestone statistics from the past.

(My perfect phrases examples won't show where I've footnoted every demographic; however, grantmakers expect you to include footnotes or endnotes, depending on the grantmaking agency's narrative formatting requirements.)

Write as much as you can about the population that you already serve.

- Buckeye Outreach for Social Services (BOSS) targets a rural, remote, and often disconnected target population. Of the more than 350 families served last year, 85% were at or below the poverty level and over 60% had less than a high school education (Annual ICP Report to Community, May 2006). According to the 2002 Census, 33% of Far West Valley residents are renters; 15.5% have no high school diplomas; 13.1% are single working parents; 29% do not speak English well; 7.4% of residents have no telephone; 16.2% earn less than $10,000 per year, 7.1% earn between $10,000 and $15,000 per year, and 10.8% earn between $15,000 and $25,000 per year; and per capita income is $15,627.

- The target population for the Cass County Even Start Initiative is unique. American Indian descendants belonging to the Pokagon Band of Potawatomi Indians, centered in Dowagiac, make up 0.8% (410 individuals) of the county's population of 51,321. African Americans constitute 6.1% (3,130) of the county's population. Cass County is ranked among the top five counties in the state for children of "some other race" (non-Hispanic only) and among the top 10 counties in the state in terms of percentage of "multi-racial children" (non-Hispanic only), according to Kids Count. While Cass County's number of children younger than 17 decreased by over 5% between 2000 and 2005, the number of *minority* children under 17 increased by 30.6%, compared with the state increase of 23.9%. Cass County is home to 33% more American Indian/Alaskan Native children than the state average.

- The Fire Safety and Education Program targets children and their families in the second largest city in Florida. One quarter of the population is of Latino origin; 24.1% of these Latinos do not speak English. Population studies (U.S. Census, 2004 projections) show that while elsewhere in the Metropolitan Statistical Area Latino immigration is slowing, in our region incoming numbers continue to rise. The fact that slightly over 26,000 households have language barriers with English is of utmost concern when it comes to child safety knowledge and understanding how to prevent injuries. The families of most people who come to the region's emergency rooms are working poor, with no insurance and with incomes at or below the federal poverty level. Research from the region's public schools and county-level planning agencies shows that there are

seven areas in the city with proportionately higher con-
centrations of non-English-speaking Latino families with
two or more children less than six years old. The percentages of Latinos in these seven areas range from 43.1% to
72.6%—much higher than in any other parts of the city.

- The youth targeted are Black, Hispanic, and Native
  American—Special Populations and Populations of
  Color—upper elementary and middle school youth who
  are already using or at risk of using alcohol, tobacco, and
  other drugs. In 2005, the Michigan Department of
  Community Health released *Assessing Substance Use
  Prevention Needs in Michigan Counties: A Study Using Social
  Indicators. Findings for Genesee County* showed Mt. Morris
  Township to be in the highest quartile of the risk rankings
  (4th). Juvenile arrest rates per 1,000 were 3.49 for liquor
  law violations, 2.77 for drug possession, 1.56 for violent
  crime, and 11.27 for property crime. All rates fall in the top
  10 for the state. In addition, the teen suicide rate, 4.36, is in
  the top five for the state. Sexual behavior, 13.71, is third
  highest in the state and family conflict is fifth highest at
  7.74. Adult crime indicators related to substance abuse
  arrests are third highest in all categories.

- The Center targets economically disadvantaged women
  residing in or near Mahoning County, the poorest county
  among Ohio's 10 largest counties (AP, 2004). Ninety percent of those served are categorized as single heads of
  household. The target population's poverty rate is almost
  seven times higher than the poverty rate of the county's
  married couples (GEOGC, 2005). Of 134,444 women in

Mahoning County, 15.3% (20,569) are living at or below the poverty rate. The women who are referred to the Center are African-American, Hispanic, and White. They are heads of their households and range in age from 18 to 60 years old, with children age one month and up. Some are grandparents caring for their grandchildren on little or no monies in the absence of parents who have long abandoned their children (due to death, incarceration, or other reasons for not actively parenting). Ten percent of the women with the program have physically challenging disabilities.

- The Runaway Youth Prevention Program targets residents in the City of Houston. Approximately 29.4% of the population is under the age of 18. It's not surprising that 49% of mothers with children under age 6 are in the labor force. The City's high school dropout rate is 19%. Forty-five percent of children under age 15 live in households that receive public assistance. In a City Kids Count 2002 survey of the 50 states conducted by the Annie E. Casey Foundation, New York City ranked 49th for percentage of children living in poverty—46%—and ranked 50th for percentage of children living in single-parent families—60%.

- The Council's target population is Minority Business Enterprises (MBEs) of all sizes, including Fortune 500 corporations, throughout the state of Illinois. An MBE is a for-profit enterprise, regardless of size, physically located in the United States or its trust territories, which is owned, operated, and controlled by "minority group members." "Minority group members" are U.S. citizens who are African American, Hispanic American, Native American,

Asian Pacific American, and Asian Indian American. Ownership by minority individuals means the business is at least 51% owned by such individuals or, in the case of a publicly owned business, at least 51% of the stock is owned by one or more such individuals. Further, the management and daily operations are controlled by those minority group members. To date, the Council has been able to target 400 certified MBEs and 70 Fortune 500 corporate members that are a strong presence in Illinois.

- The District's target population includes 32,000 students from kindergarten through grade 12. The student population is 31% Anglo, 49% Hispanic, 13% Asian, 3% Black, and 4% other. Nearly 30% of the students have limited English proficiency; up to 53.8% of families are foreign-born, and up to 69% do not speak English well.

- The target population resides in the Fifth Ward. This neighborhood is the nucleus of Prospect's inner city and a visible testament to the city's problems. Approximately 750 individuals live in our immediate neighborhood: 244 households with 166 families. There are 189 children ages 3 to 12 years old enrolled in school. The median income for families is $17,917, well below the county and state median income levels. Of the children targeted for our programs, 25% are learning disabled, approximately 30% are ADHD, and 10% are emotionally or physically impaired.

- The target population for the Johnsonville Chapter of the National Organ Donor Alliance is healthy individuals who are between the ages of 21 and 45 years old and drug-free, not using either illegal or legal substances.

Regretfully, this provision often reduces our pool of acceptable donors 40% or more. Individuals taking prescription medications, smoking or chewing tobacco products, or drinking alcohol are eliminated from the donor database. Rigorous medical screening determines if they are disease-free and healthy enough to donate an organ. Seventy-five percent of donors in the database have indicated their willingness to donate a kidney. The remaining 25% of registered donors have committed to donate all of their useable organs to a transplant candidate or to a scientific research institution.

2. Demonstrate Their Roles as Stakeholders in Your Proposed Program

Grantmaking agencies also want to know how your target population has been, is currently, and will be actively involved in impacting the decisions made by your organization. This is the section of the target population narrative where you show that your organization is not operating in a tunnel—making critical decisions that will impact people who have not provided input at any level. These perfect phrases will also give you ideas about how to involve your target population in multiple areas of planning, advising, and evaluating your grant-funded programs.

- **Pre-Proposal Planning Involvement:** A public meeting was held in early June for the community at large, including parents from the participating sites, former mentors from the federally funded U.S. Department of Justice Juvenile Mentoring Program (JUMP), and former and current volunteers from other programs. In total, over 100 individuals participated in the pre-proposal planning process and voiced their continuing commitment to be available as resources for the proposed mentoring program. The implementation plan, as well as the monitoring and evaluation plans, also calls for stakeholder input and participation.

- **Pre-Proposal Planning Involvement:** When Doctors Without Walls publicly announced that it would apply for National Institutes of Health grant funds, calls and e-mails came in from around the world with documented needs statements and program design ideas. Twenty international conference calls were announced on our Web site in a "call for input." Medical professionals and patients from 45 countries in need of our services participated in the calls. Their responses were loud and clear and resulted in what we feel is a highly competitive grant application narrative for the Institutes' Global Health Response Initiative.

- **Committee Level Involvement:** The CPS Strategic Technology Committee members represent school staff, parents, business leaders, regional colleges, libraries, and community leaders. These individuals have been working on the committee for several years and are active throughout the district. The district stakeholders wrote the Technology Plan and evaluated its progress. This grant application reflects the needs of the entire stakeholder community, not just CPS employees.

- **Committee Level Involvement:** Raisin Charter Township recreational facilities are administered by a seven-member Parks Committee. These members are local residents who volunteer their time. The Committee is responsible for the maintenance, operation, policies, and preparation of the budget for Mitchell Park. These elements are adopted and/or approved by the Township Board of Trustees. The Raisin Charter Township Board, Planning Commission, and the Parks Committee worked cooperatively to create a 2005–2010 Raisin Charter Township Parks Master Plan. In 2004, the Parks Committee surveyed residents of Raisin Township to evaluate their needs. Nearly 60% of the survey forms were returned and identified the residents' desire to improve Mitchell Park as a top priority. Furthermore, the Raisin Charter Township Parks Committee identified critical needs at Mitchell Park by observed deficiencies and desires provided by area soccer clubs and Little League teams.

- **Advisory Council Involvement:** The Consortium recognizes that target population participation is key to the project's success. Once the participants are attending the weekly Risk Awareness Training sessions, the Coordinator will work with each member agency to identify those participants interested in forming a Stakeholders' Advisory Council. The Council will be a grassroots vehicle for providing the Consortium with feedback from end users about service and public education needs within the target population in the county.

- **Advisory Council Involvement:** At the Parent Preview Night last year, parents of the targeted middle school adolescents were asked to volunteer for the Adolescent Family Life (AFL) Advisory Council. The Council members include parents, ministers from churches and other faith-based groups in each school community, health care practitioners, and anyone else representing the public who is interested in and supportive of the Sex Can Wait approach to abstinence. Their attendance rates have been high and their feedback has been critical to the program's direction.

- **Evaluation Plan Involvement:** All stakeholders will be involved in the data samplings and reporting. Interim and final evaluation reports will be provided to participant groups in debriefing forums, to Advisory Board members (each program will have an Advisory Board made up of representatives from community partners and the stake-holders group), and to funding agencies.

■ **Evaluation Plan Involvement:** Upon completion of each training class, participants were asked to fill out forms to evaluate the program and the facilities. Year after year, comments that are entered in the written comment area express the need for more courses, greater frequency of courses, and more room to accommodate individuals on the waiting lists. Their direct input has resulted in adding new courses and offering them in more time slots. In Year 1, the waiting list for courses was six months long. This year, no one is on the waiting list and all classes are full.

3. Show Funders How Target Population Input Impacts Strategic Planning

By now you are beginning to understand just how involved funders expect your target population or stakeholders to be in providing input. Your organization best demonstrates its process of getting and using input from end users when it opens its doors, vision, and mission for public scrutiny and feedback and incorporates the input into its long-range strategic plan.

- During the development process for the town's General Development Long-Range Strategic Plan in the 1980s and its subsequent update in 2001, multiple public input meetings were held to garner feedback on how to best preserve the heritage of the town for its residents. In 1998, 70 community members met to develop the Plan. At that time, a 15-member Planning Committee was created. The Committee reviewed research on historic preservation and Central Business District revitalization. In 2001, when the town's General Development Plan was updated, a series of public planning workshops were held. At the visioning workshop, broad community aspirations were discussed and downtown development goals and objectives were created. In three additional public meetings, the historic preservation issues were discussed and public feedback was sought. Public hearings were conducted by the Development Board and the town council. These public input sessions resulted in Long-Range Strategic Plan refinements and the implementation design presented in this grant application.

Target Population

- The state Department of Technology Innovation is the largest stakeholder in small business innovation research and technology transfer projects. During the public meeting phase required under this competitive grant application for technology innovation research, five key staff persons from the state agency and 27 industry-related project managers were in attendance. Their overall concern, requests for additional information, and sincere comments related to concept improvement were invaluable to our strategic business planning process. This venture is costing our company $4.5 million. We cannot afford to operate under a bubble; it is critical that public input be incorporated into this product. These potential end users and technology experts have significantly impacted the direction our company will take in researching and developing this emerging technological device.

- While Meals on Wheels could continue to make major decisions from within the organization about delivery zones and times and meal contents, it has historically relied on the clients who benefit most from our daily nutritional supplements. Their feedback is critical when it comes to preferred delivery times, services when a resident moves out of zone, and the types of foods clients want included in the daily balance of nourishment. Our organization recently completed its 10th long-range strategic plan (three years of forecasting). The impact of public input lessened the guessing and stressing normally associated with this process in the past.

Standing Rules for Content Length for Various Formats

Remember: the length of your response for this narrative section is determined by the grantmaking agency's published guidelines. Government grants will always be lengthy, allowing you to write multiple paragraphs for each narrative section. Private sector funders want to read less and they force you to write in brief and concise paragraphs.

Chapter 5
Community Served and Partners:
Providing Insight on Your Service Region and Collaborations

Many of your grant proposals will be sent to grantmakers who are not located in your state. This means that the program staff or peer reviewers who read about your organization may not be familiar with its location or region. Therefore, it's critical that you give the readers a virtual tour of the organization's service region.

This next collection of perfect phrases will take you on many virtual tours to help you understand why the reader must "connect" to your location before positive funding decisions will be made. Once you've learned how to acquaint funders with your service area, I'll give you some great perfect phrases for introducing your key partners and their roles and for presenting an award-winning networking strengths statement.

Elements of a Winning Community Served and Partners Section:

1. Acquaint Funders with Your Service Area.
2. Introduce Your Key Partners and Their Roles in Grant-Funded Programs.
3. Provide Funders with an Accurate Description of Your Organization's Collaborative Networking Strengths.

1. Acquaint Funders with Your Service Area

Some grantmakers will not ask for this specific narrative section. In their narrative writing instructions, it may be incorporated into a Strategies or Approaches section. Whether you are asked to write several sentences or several pages, this section will help you understand what they are looking for when they request information on your service area.

- Boscobel Area Medical Center's service region includes nine rural southwestern Wisconsin counties and one rural northeastern Iowa county bordering Wisconsin. The total population of the service area is 125,000. The region's economy is flat, but steady due to the high number of agribusiness operations, public sector employers (largest payroll statistics for the region), retail chains, and Indian gaming casinos.

- The Sanibel Island Improvement Association's service region encompasses 54 square miles off the west coast of Florida, three miles out from Fort Myers Beach. There are 1,350 residents and over 5,000 seasonal visitors. The island is home to a Navy observation station and diving practice area (10 miles of restricted coastal waters), a nature conservatory, small retail shops, one grocery store, and a medical clinic. Access to Sanibel Island is limited to small planes and boats and to motor vehicles via the Sanibel Causeway.

- The Carlsbad Cavern Museum is a part of the Carlsbad Cavern National Park located in New Mexico's Guadalupe Mountains. Annually, Park and Museum visitors come from 50 states and over two dozen countries. The Museum has a patron mailing list with 453,000 names (collected over a 40-year timeframe). We are amazed at the continuing interest in our geological exploration areas.

- Third-Fifth Bank Foundation operates in 18 states. Service regions are generally in urban areas with populations over 500,000. Currently, the majority of our locations are east of the Mississippi River. The Foundation awards grants in the communities where the 187 branches are located. Collectively, the communities served have over 1,200 non-profit organizations.

- The Southwest Iowa Library's Service area includes 19 counties and over three dozen public libraries. The service region encompasses 459 square miles. Over 20% of the area is remote—rural, isolated, and not on a major state thoroughfare; the remainder is urban and suburban. In some areas, one small public library serves multiple counties.

- The West Virginia Public Service Commission service region is the entire state, from mountainous terrain to bottom of the valley mining communities. The Commission must travel monthly to hold public utilities hearings across the state. Within the service region, there are hundreds of private and public utility providers that fall under our jurisdiction. Due to the stagnant economy and historically high poverty rates, public opinion is most needed when a local utility provider requests a rate increase.

- The Peoria Boxing Club's service region encompasses six South Side communities. The Club is a seven-day-per-week home to over 600 aspiring boxers of all ages. Our urban locale with nearby parks and sports stadiums is a magnet for youth and their families.

- Fairview Charter School serves 500 families in and adjacent to El Dorado, Arkansas. The service region is limited to Union County. Even without marketing and outreach to our neighbor to the south, 20 of the 500 students enrolled at the school come from Union Parish, Louisiana. Fairview's service region takes in 100 square miles of pristine forest land that has been over-harvested by the logging industry. The region is also home to Arkansas' largest oil and natural gas exploration corporation. The school is located on U.S. 82, a major east-west thoroughfare.

- Newspapers for the Blind serves 10,000 visually impaired persons throughout the United States and abroad. As a nonprofit governmental organization founded in the United Kingdom, the service region has grown beyond our original vision—serving European Union states that lacked technologically advanced services for the visually impaired. Approximately 20% of those served reside in Latin America, Canada, the European Union, and South Pacific islands.

- The Rainbow Region Community Action Program (CAP) serves 4,536 Washington State residents living in three northern counties bordering Canada. The service region is located in the foothills of the largest mountain range in North America. The 9,000-foot elevation of most of the service region means highly dangerous conditions for our mobile library services. The region has an average of 300 days of rain, fog, and near-blizzard conditions that result in large blocks of isolation for the residents served by the CAP.

- One House, One Family, Inc. serves individuals and families seeking to relocate to the Burnside Neighborhood Development area in Toronto's inner city. The service region is made up of nearly 500 aging homes built circa 1900. Burnside was once a prestigious upscale neighborhood of gingerbread houses that hosted annual holiday open houses for the public. Today, 50% of the houses in this neighborhood are vacant because of code violations and owner/renter abandonment.

- The Roadside Refuge service area is 336 miles long and encompasses all of I-40 within Oklahoma, beginning at the Arkansas border and ending at the Texas Panhandle border. On any given day, Roadside Refuge helps stranded regional and national travelers make emergency calls to have a vehicle towed or to have a family member or a friend picked up. The service region counts over 4 million vehicles yearly that use this heavily trafficked Interstate to drive across the country.

2. Introduce Your Key Partners and Their Roles in Grant-Funded Programs

Now, I'm going to show you how to introduce key partners and their roles using the same organizations as in the first section of this chapter.

- The Center's key partners and their roles are:
  1. Friends of the Boscobel Area Medical Center—Functions as the 501 (c)(3) fundraising arm and fiscal agent for the Center's grant proposals. Responsible for raising matching funds, when needed, by holding special community events that produce revenues.
  2. State of Wisconsin Department of Health—Functions as the jurisdictional licensing agency for the Center's public health clinics. Links the Center's clinic-level evaluation process with the statewide evaluation for federal reporting purposes.

- The Association's key partners and their roles are:
  1. U.S. Navy—Provides research data on the Island's indigenous underwater species. This information helps the Association promote its preservation message and attracts marine biologists from around the world to spend time on the Island.
  2. State of Florida Department of Environmental Protection—Assists in preserving the Island's fragile habitat and helps to monitor all commercial development and ocean explorations.

- The Museum's key partners and their roles are:
  1. U.S. Department of the Interior National Park Service—

Helps to promote the Museum's presence worldwide by including a link on its high-hit Web site.

2. State of New Mexico Council for the Humanities—Supports visitor education programs with funding and advertising. Enables public schools to make field trips from throughout New Mexico to the Museum by funding Arts on the Move grant applications. Encourages New Mexico's postsecondary institutions to conduct historic studies at the Park and use the Museum as a knowledge base.

- The Foundation has multiple stakeholders. Among them, we count these high-profile organizations as key partners in achieving our grant-funded program goals and objectives:
  1. American Council on Foundations—Provides administrative management training and connectivity to other U.S.-based corporate foundations. Helps the Foundation to adhere to the IRS guidelines for corporate foundation giving and assets monitoring.
  2. American Banking Association—Offers oversight for corporate social investment initiatives to ensure they meet with national standards under the Banking Association's regulatory guidelines.

- The Library Service's partners and their roles include:
  1. Iowa Department of Library Services—Provides professional development training, facilitates collections inventories and manages the statewide accessible database for each library in the system, and links libraries in need of volunteers, materials and supplies, and furnishings and equipment with corporate grantmakers.

2. County Boards of Commissioners—Provides the Library Service with access to matching funds in 19 counties. Each Commission sets aside up to $50,000 annually for matching fund grant requests submitted by the Library Service. The Commission also provides meeting space in each county to accommodate community feedback meetings or some of the public meetings required by government grantmaking agencies.

- The West Virginia Public Service Commission's partners and their roles are:

  1. Public Utilities Foundation—Enables the Commission to receive annual competitive grant funds for statewide education programs and marketing-related travel. Since 2000, the Foundation has awarded $700,000 to the Commission to fulfill its public expectations. The Foundation also sponsored the national Utilities Commission Conference, which was held in Wheeling in 2006. This support ($84,000) was in addition to the Commission's annual grant award (averaging $100,000).

  2. Governor's Office on Strategic Planning—Assists the Commission in fine-tuning its long-range goals and objectives relating to its role in business and industry. Provides the Commission with a shared lobbyist who works as a liaison with the West Virginia Congressional team. Underwrites the cost to operate the Commission's cable television broadcast of all public meetings.

- Community partners for the Peoria Boxing Club are (asset-building roles included):

  1. Illinois Sports Commission—Provides licensing and

accreditation for the Club. Promotes the Club's presence and purpose nationally from its high-profile state Web site. Works with the juvenile justice courts in multiple counties to facilitate referrals for high-risk, court-involved youth to the Club. Allows the use of its name in all marketing materials developed and distributed by the Club. Assigns a key staff member to attend all publicized events and monitor Commission compliance.

2. Joe Jefferson Ministries—Helps to market the Club to faith-based groups in its weekly televised broadcast on the FBN network. Encourages all youth in the listening audience to visit and join our Club or one in their own state or community. Solicits online donations for the Club and sends a check four times a year. The average annual contribution from Joe Jefferson Ministries is $25,000. The organization has supported the Club for 10 years.

■ The Fairview Charter School has many partners. Here is an abbreviated list of our key partners and their role in supporting our mission and vision:

1. El Dorado Unified School District—Co-sponsored the charter school application process and agreed to provide fiscal oversight with Southern Arkansas University. Extends invitations for all professional development programs to enable Fairview staff to attend at no charge. Provides technical assistance for the annual state standardized testing process required for all Arkansas students and taken by four grade levels.

2. Regional Transportation Association—Works with Fairview to provide affordable transportation for fami-

lies whose children must be picked up and dropped off at home or an after-school child care provider. Enables children from throughout Union County, Arkansas, and Union Parish, Louisiana, to attend our charter school.

- Newspapers for the Blind has cultivated several long-term partners with significant international influence. The list below offers a brief overview of these entities and their role in our continuing success.

  1. United Kingdom Reading Programme—Provides hundreds of volunteer readers annually for the newspaper recording component at Newspapers for the Blind. Maintains a database of volunteers with updated contact information and the hours volunteered each month. Promotes the service to visually impaired persons via public service announcements on its weekly international broadcast via Radio Liberty. Helps our organization plan and carry out an annual volunteer appreciation programme.

  2. United Nations Commission for the Disabled—Supports our organization by giving it international visibility among potential donors. Using United Nations Foundations funds, the Commission works as an advocate with foreign ministries in undeveloped countries to encourage their support and obtain guaranteed access for visually impaired beneficiaries.

- Partners and their roles for the Rainbow Region CAP are:

  1. Rainbow Valley Food Bank—Coordinates the information and referral process for low-income individuals served by them who are also in need of CAP services.

Holds an annual winter clothing drive to help CAP families who do not have clothing sufficient to survive in brutally cold winters. Helps CAP make its annual appeal and report to the state's Agency for the Poor. Joins CAP in its annual health fair, which draws over 5,000 regional visitors and helps distribute our literature. Coordinates food basket distribution with the CAP mobile library vans.

2. Association of Northern Washington Librarians—Provides contract and volunteer librarians for CAP mobile service vans twice monthly. Librarians sign up new library patrons, issue them a card, and help them choose their first three books. The Association also develops parent/child reading programs in rural locales and provides a librarian to set up the program and train parents to be peer leaders in order to sustain all activities in the region.

■ One House, One Family has several unique partners that provide multiple enhancements to our program's abilities:

1. Ruth Watson Carter Charitable Trust—Has provided executives on loan and over $500,000 in grant awards to jump-start the redevelopment of 25 historical homes. Supports all neighborhood initiatives by either contributing additional monies or sending liberal press releases to the Province's main newspapers. Annually recognizes the efforts of individual families who help restore their new homes by giving them gift coupons for home furnishings, appliances, landscaping materials, and security systems. Pays for Province-approved historical preservation architects to work on each home (out-

side of traditional grant funding) to ensure that all renovations are in compliance with preservation codes.
Publishes the monthly Canadian Housing Preservation
magazine and allows one of our volunteers to write a
monthly "home and family" column to promote One
House, One Family efforts.

2. Toronto Housing Authority—Works with our organization to ensure that code violations are corrected before
volunteers begin on each home. Works hand in hand
with the preservation architects to ensure that all
changes or updates meet with the City inspector's
approval. Helps our organization meet all regulatory
compliances.

- The Roadside Refuge has been historically privileged in its
partnership commitments. Our partners include:

1. Oklahoma Department of Public Safety—Provides
instant communications about road closures, lane
restrictions, and major traffic incidents so our service
volunteers can respond expeditiously. Works with us to
train staff and volunteers in handling hostile motorists.
Provides each vehicle with a scanner and maintains the
scanners at no cost to our organization. Sponsors 20
billboard advertisements along Interstate 40 to notify
motorists of our service and give them the 800 emergency assistance telephone number. Alerts motorists of
our official vehicle decal and ID badges so that they will
not cooperate with impersonators who could endanger
the lives of those stranded and waiting for roadside
assistance.

2. Automobile Association of Oklahoma (AAO)—Publicizes our services to its 40,000 members in Oklahoma. Distributes a window decal with our toll-free number for members to place on their vehicles. Spotlights a feedback column in its monthly AAO Safe Driver Magazine for individuals who have received our road-side services. Donates $1 for every member ordering extra window decals (selling for $2 each on the AAO Web site) and sends an annual contribution to our organization. Over the past 20 years, AAO contributions have totaled $200,000.

3. Provide Funders with an Accurate Description of Your Organization's Collaborative Networking Strengths

It's time to tout the strong points of your relationship with community partners. This is really all about how well your organization networks to maximize its internal resources.

■ The Center was instrumental in establishing a region-wide health care consortium. As the lead agency, we have been able to engage politically different, geographically spread health care providers, medical staffing services, and medical professionals in forum-type conversations about the quality of health care. The consortium's success in reducing service duplications and developing a patient database accessible by those members providing direct services has propelled it to the forefront of national health care reform.

■ The Association's partners credit our due diligence process in protecting Sanibel Island. Whenever there is any hint of environmental endangerment, a core group of environmental lawyers immediately files an injunction to block the parties in question. This quick and aggressive move on the part of the Association has helped it win the support and sustaining partnership of rigid and highly respected national environmental rights groups. These groups now look to the Association for policy tracking, Congressional testimonies, and public demonstrations to prevent commercialization of protected properties and species.

■ The Museum has taken the lead in multiple state-level history education programs. Working with our network of National Parks Education Advisors, we were able to develop a template of the main educational points that each Park should offer in a visitor education program. The National Association of Natural History Journalists has joined our National Advisory Council for State Park Museums. This new partner promises to bring the needs and accomplishments for our Museum to a high level of public awareness.

- The Foundation is the leading mid-size banking charity in the United States. Partners in the financial industry and from among the large group of banking corporate grant-makers have asked the Foundation to act as the fiscal agent and lead grant applicant for the U.S. Department of Commerce's Spread the Wealth Initiative. As the lead partner with multiple high-profile partners committed to higher levels of social responsibility, the Foundation expects to apply for a $1 million multi-state grant.

- The Library is one of 60 regional libraries that have formed a Web partnership to enable electronic document access for the federal government's document depository. The depository holders meet four times per year at the Southwest Iowa Library Service District headquarters to evaluate customer feedback, storage limitations, and Web-related issues. Our partnership has been recognized by the Governor's Office for its high customer satisfaction levels.

- The West Virginia Public Service Commission has been selected by the National Public Utilities Association to lead the 50 states in developing a national Web site with links to all of the state commissions. In addition, the Association has appointed the President of our commission to serve on the national board for three years. This honor will enable the West Virginia Public Service Commission to become one of the nation's leading public utilities entities. While past partnerships have been very beneficial, this new level of partnering with high-profile associations will strengthen West Virginia's statewide capabilities to monitor and manage public and private utilities.

■ The Club belongs to a 40-member coalition serving youth. Our membership has raised awareness of the Club's presence and purpose in the service region. The coalition has helped the Club expand its outreach efforts to include youth living in foster homes and public housing complexes. In addition, the coalition has helped the Club travel to Washington, DC, and testify before Congress about the ongoing issues impacting high-risk youth and the need for community-based youth development programs. This testimony resulted in six new federal-level grantmaking programs targeting youth development initiatives.

■ Among its many partners, the Fairview Charter School considers itself the leading agency for all of southern Arkansas' public charter schools. When the state Department of Education cut charter school funding by $5 million statewide, our group of 18 schools demonstrated in front of the House of Representatives Fiscal Agency building in Little Rock and won back $3.5 million of the funding cut.

■ The Director for Newspapers for the Blind serves on the

European Union's Council of NGOs. This prestigious appointment by the Prime Minister of Great Britain enables our organization to have multi-country influence and visibility. Other NGOs serving special populations have sought out Newspapers for the Blind for advice and advocacy at the governmental level.

- The CAP is a part of a national network of 155 CAPs that work collaboratively to serve the underserved in the United States. This network is the largest social programs partnership in North America. We are able to leverage commodity purchasing, benefit from an intra-CAP employee hiring service, and move surplus commodity inventories across state lines in record time.

- The Roadside Refuge Service would not be able to operate efficiently or effectively without its multiple partners in Oklahoma. Many service groups, like Civitan and Kiwanis, help refer volunteers to our organization. The Area Agency on Aging has partnered with us statewide to provide regional volunteer-run call centers to receive emergency requests for roadside assistance.

Remember: the funder's guidelines will dictate the length of your narrative response when you are covering the community served and partnership.

Part Two

**Perfect Phrases for
the Description
of Your Request**

Chapter 6
Problem or Need:
Conveying the Urgency of the Situation in Need of Grant Funding

This is the grant proposal narrative section that you've been eager to write ever since you started reading *Perfect Phrases for Writing Grant Proposals*. Now that you've learned how to build a solid organization introduction and background, it's time to start developing the problems and needs of your target population.

I want to forewarn you that this is not the narrative section where you jump into writing about the solutions to the problem. It is the section where you present the problems or needs in compelling, story-like sentences and paragraphs that draw the reader in slowly but surely. I have so much fun creating these paragraphs that I know you will quickly catch on and start writing your own phrases.

Use a **bold** font to emphasize your most dire information about the situation. Also, remember to cite all of your statistics. For space constraints, I have not incorporated citations into every paragraph.

Elements of a Winning Narrative Section:

1. Use Statistics to Build Your Case for Grant Funding.
2. State Facts with Emotion.
3. Provide Funders with Financial Facts to Support the Request.

1. Use Statistics to Build Your Case for Grant Funding

You can find the statistics needed to build these perfect phrases in your organization's past surveys, questionnaires, or needs assessments of its target population. Data collections on your target population's problems are essential when it comes to having the "right" statistics in each of your paragraphs.

- In 2006, Classical Ensemble conducted a survey of audience demographics. Over the course of 10 public performances held at venues in ethnic neighborhoods, volunteers interviewed patrons to inquire about their ethnicity and musical preferences. We also asked where they lived and how far they traveled to attend one of our performances. The results showed the following. **Fewer than 10%** of all Classical Ensemble audience members are minorities. While the performances are held at churches, schools, and community centers in ethnic neighborhoods, **90% of the people attending them traveled 10 or more miles from non-minority areas/neighborhoods to attend**. Overwhelmingly, **100% of those surveyed** indicated a love for classical music. Clearly, our efforts to bring this age-old musical genre to underrepresented audience groups are missing the mark!

- Traffic accidents are one of the fastest-growing causes of sudden death and disability in developing countries. The World Health Organization estimates that by 2020 road accidents will be the **world's third leading cause of pre-**

mature death for all ages. On average, **20% of all people killed in traffic accidents in developing countries are under age 15**. This is **twice as high** as in the developed world. In countries where motorbikes are the primary mode of transportation, **95% of accidents involve head injuries—20% are fatal; 80% debilitating**.

- Young male high school students in Carson City, Nevada are not graduating at the same rates as their female classmates. For the past three years, **high school freshmen and juniors have had an average dropout rate of 17% annually**. The lure of nearby manual labor or service sector work is taking these potential scholars from classroom seats to the dangers of the mines and to the neon lights of casinos. According to the U.S. Department of Education, **the lifetime earning capacity of a high school dropout is 500% less than that of a high school graduate!**

- The Helena Cattle Cooperative has **lost over 12% of its herd** (5,000 cattle) to avoidable diseases in the past three years. Our research division has been aggressively trying to develop a vaccine to prevent hoof-and-mouth disease— the **number-one cause of death** for cattle worldwide! Over 1 million cattle die from this dreaded and fast-spreading disease annually. Three years ago the Federal Drug Administration was petitioned to approve a vaccine. While waiting for this needed clearance, an **additional 2,000 cattle have died** in our region from this deadly disease.

- St. Raphael's Roman Catholic Church in Crossover, Georgia, has **600 parishioners—and seating for only 100**. This sudden growth is due to the development of a subdivision that has added 1,200 single-family homes and a 100-unit senior citizens apartment complex. The **demand for additional services has stretched our creativity beyond the walls of the church**. We have expanded our weekend services from one Sunday morning Mass to one Mass on Saturday afternoon and five Masses on Sunday. Our capacity is stretched to the point where we've started holding a Sunday noon Mass outdoors in a canvas tent in order to seat the nearly 200 participants.

- Northern Oregon Rescue **responded to 3,500 calls** for mountain rescues last year. **Over 80% of rescues involved mountain retrievals** of stranded hikers **and water retrievals** for overturned rafters. These calls have taken their toll on our small volunteer staff. The **turnover rate of volunteers has been 92%**—and it's a costly number in terms of training and retaining new volunteers. The demand for our services has long exceeded our human resources. **Morale is at an all-time low** with the handful of seasoned volunteers left to conduct rescues.

- The reservation's population has been **dwindling by 5% per year** over the past decade. We are losing our **youth, who represent 90% of the members leaving the reservation and losing all contact with tribal officials**. The other **10% are the tribal elders**, who are **dying at record levels** from kidney and liver failure and cardiovascular disease. Of chief concern are the **1,500 families remaining on the reservation** without the benefit of wisdom from the elders and with many children, grandchildren, brothers, and sisters living elsewhere, whereabouts unknown.

- In the first quarter of this year, **700 senior citizens participated in the enrichment programs** at the Mercury Valley Senior Center in North Dakota. Of this number, **20% were in wheelchairs**. The Center has two entrances; only one is handicapped accessible. This door is at the front of our building where we have the most walk-in traffic. Because the **front entrance is over 1,000 feet from the classroom and common meeting room**, the buses carrying the seniors in wheelchairs must drive around to the back—near their classrooms and the main meeting room—where **there is only a single door, with an elevated threshold, not accessible to wheelchairs**. At that entrance, seniors have to be lifted out of their chairs by our staff and carried across the threshold. The Center's administrative offices and private screening/counseling cubicles take up all of the space at the front of the building. We cannot change the building's setup because the Center is **50 years old** and these renovations have **been overlooked for nearly a decade** because our location is rural and because our seniors have not complained much.

- The San Juan Housing Authority must cope with an unappealing exterior. The Authority's **375 multi-family units** were **built 15 years ago** with a federal housing grant. Families move here as a last resort—it's a bleak alternative to homelessness. The concrete gray buildings are anything but homelike. Our concern is that their outside appearance **shows a lack of pride and conveys the message that they are low-income and visually depressing public housing units**. What's missing? Grass, flowers, shrubs, trees, brick pavers, and basic landscaping in general. For the **past 10 years**, our administrators have ordered **500 tons of landscape rocks** to cover the muddy front and back yards. Much to our amazement, there has been a critical shortage of any type of rocks on our island—leaving our complexes **stark and barren**.

- Red River Parish, Louisiana, has been **without its Tourism and Convention Director and its Economic Development Director for 13 years!** During this time, the Parish's **new business development has dropped 65%.** We used to host six international conventions annually that brought **over $5 million** in revenues into the Parish. When these two positions were vacated, the Parish board voted not to replace the directors. The board members felt that Red River could sell itself! With no new businesses or major conventions, we've had **no significant job growth!**

2. State Facts with Emotion

Don't hold back now! Let the emotions flow—you must convince the people who are going to decide on funding your grant proposal that you're in dire need of their monies!

■ The Board of Directors is **gravely concerned** about the financial stability of the Classical Ensemble. The **ongoing costs** of providing public performances, extending our educational outreach, and attracting new, more diverse audiences have **simply surpassed our revenue-raising abilities**. We have tried to spread the word about our concerts; but at this time we have only a handful of volunteers to answer the telephone and sell tickets. There is **no money** for major advertising and our educational outreach must rely solely on the Artistic Director, who visits schools in his spare time. **Most importantly, our small nonprofit group lacks the know-how and staffing to tap into the minority audience market**. Rocky Mountain Valley demographics tell us that we are missing hundreds of potential paying audience members and ongoing contributors.

■ **Asia is where the problem is the worst—on the verge of becoming a childhood epidemic**. Nearly one-half of the world's road deaths occur in Asia. As poor economies globalize, more money means more motorbikes. Greater usage of motorbikes means more crashes, further straining already overburdened health systems and aggravating poverty. Walk through the public hospital wards on any day and you'll find **dozens of young patients with their heads swathed in bandages, necks secured with**

braces, or heads anchored in steel halos. These young daredevils would rather ride their motorbikes with no helmets than to put on traditional "rice cooker" helmets!

■ It could be your son or daughter choosing to give up the benefits of a high school diploma! Would you simply give up and let your teenager drop out of school? Would you avoid conflict and simply support his or her choice? Fifty years ago, you could drop out of high school and walk into a job that paid livable wages and offered some hope for future advancements. **Those days are over—the American dream has turned into a mountain of uncertainty for those without a high school diploma**. In our community, far too many young male students are falling through the "school retention counseling" gaps!

■ Across America and throughout the rest of the world, **vaccines that could reduce mass deaths among cattle are being held hostage** by antiquated government review-and-approval systems. Human subject trials can last from seven to 10 years. However, for animals, the wait is even longer—sometimes indefinite. On average, it takes nearly 15 years for a new animal vaccine to be approved in the U.S. and abroad. **By the time a vaccine is approved for mass distribution, the disease has often mutated into a vaccine-resistant strand of genetic molecules**. Our Research Division has perfected a vaccine that will prevent dreaded hoof-and-mouth disease. However, **it does not have the funds needed to conduct the final stage of Federal Drug Administration testing**.

■ The church has gone as far as to build a removable side

wall so that when we have a large wedding or funeral all guests can be accommodated. This plan works well during the summers; however, during the cold winters and rainy springs, removing a wall for open air seating is not an option. **On 29 occasions in the past year, we've had to move weddings and funerals to the nearby high school gymnasium**. Each move is **cumbersome** for members of our congregations and our guests and **embarrassing** for the people who try to serve them.

- Imagine helping out in a mountain rescue. You receive an alert at home via beeper, you drive to the station, and you get ready to suit up and load your gear—only to find that you're the only volunteer responding to the call to save lives! The volunteer attrition rate has been an overwhelming burden for the few dedicated core volunteers who started Northern Oregon Rescue three years ago. We never dreamed that just wanting to help individuals lost, hurt, or disoriented on our mountains and in our rivers and streams would be so hard. **Each rescue call should inspire adrenaline-powered hope. Instead, each call generates a dark cloud of fear and inadequacy!**

- The Tribe's **heritage and future are slipping away** at the same time and it's painful for those members who remain on the reservation. **Hope** for continuing to teach our native language to our young ones **is diminishing**. Dreams for our elders to live their final days in peace and harmony have been replaced by **nightmares of illness, freezing during cold winters, and abandonment by younger family members**. Family preservation efforts are an unfunded priority. Yes, it's a sad Tribal reality—we make families our priority, yet we lack the funding to preserve our family life and rituals.

- The State Department on Disabilities has visited our Center annually and cited us for failing to have a handicapped accessible rear door. This same Department has **turned down our grant requests for ADA-compliance renovations the past five years**. We have repeatedly asked for funds to renovate the Center's back entrance to include a ramp and a double automatic door and to widen the 500-foot back hallway to accommodate wheelchair users. We expect the Center's enrichment classes to **double over the next two years**. This expectation stems from the recent announcement that Bismarck Health Systems is going to build a **400-unit senior citizens apartment complex and a 40-unit Alzheimer's unit within five miles of the Center**.

- Public housing has always carried an **enduring stigma**. When the average person thinks of living in a subsidized multi-family setting, he or she remembers the 1970s sitcom Good Times, where public housing was depicted as **crime-ridden, crowded, and only for "those" people!** In Puerto Rico, we believe that public housing has come a long way or at least has entered a new paradigm. However, our beliefs are hard to maintain when we drive up and see **the stark dark brown muddy lawns**. We've actually given up on ever getting the landscaping rocks needed to cover the bare areas. At this point, our Authority Board would rejoice at a truckload of grass seed and flower seeds. Is this too much to ask for **hardworking families who are struggling to put food on their tables and educate their families?**

- Here's a snapshot of Red River Parish today. Many established **businesses have closed**. Three school districts have consolidated and **reduced their teaching and support staffs by 60%**. Four **public health clinics have been boarded up**. Most of the Parish's middle-income families have moved to an adjacent parish that has a new housing development, new schools, and a new parish government center. Red River Parish was once a beautiful place to visit and live. A **few misguided elected officials chose to cut the administrative budget** in order to fulfill their campaign promises. **Can the economic damage be repaired?**

3. Provide Funders with Financial Facts to Support the Request

The research you include in the grant proposal narrative can be related to your target population (in a request for program funding) or your organization (in a request for general operating support).

- For the past three years, grants have ranged from $50,000 from the Northern Tree Foundation (whose president is chairman of Classical Ensemble) to $20,000 from the International Institute for Classical Music to $10,000 from individual board members. However, this infusion of mostly personal funding has been exhausted. Our most recent concert season was the toughest ever, financially, in the history of Classical Ensemble. The Board of Directors is gravely concerned about the financial stability of Classical Ensemble. The costs of providing public performances, extending our educational outreach, and attracting new, more diverse audiences have surpassed the Ensemble's revenue-raising abilities. **With internal sources of revenue exhausted, we must focus on building larger and more diverse audiences**.

- The Safety First Asian Initiative has distributed helmets to riders ages 15 and younger for the past five years. **Each year, it has been a struggle to manufacture durable and appealing helmets that Asian adolescents were willing to wear.** We have finally perfected a lightweight, air flow, comfortable, attractive, yet durable product. The Ministry of Transportation has committed $500,000 (U.S.)

to underwrite the cost of manufacturing and free distribution to riders ages 15 and younger; however, **this money has been slow in coming—leaving us in dire financial straits**. Politics have taken precedence over saving young lives. We are at a standstill, with no production occurring at the Vietnam manufacturing facility.

- The Carson City Community Foundation cannot solve the problem alone. Yes, it is a problem when there are no other community agencies working to reduce the dropout rate of male high school students in Nevada's state capital. Every service provider in Carson City has a mission to save lives—the lives of families, young children, single mothers, and the elderly. Other than our Foundation, **no one else seems to realize that our older teens are in trouble**. There has been very little funding available from the private or public sectors to address this problem. **Our meager allocation of $25,000 per year to work with troubled teens is simply not enough!**

- The Helena Cattle Cooperative has only 112 members—all working cattle farms in the central Montana valley region. Collectively, our farms produce gross revenues in excess of $10 million annually. However, after expenses—of which the highest are veterinarian bills and mass cattle burial expenses—profits are nonexistent! The average dairy cow is valued at $3,000. **Over the lifetime of its expected milk production, one cow can bring in 100 times its value to the owner**. When cows die suddenly and an entire herd is quarantined, cooperative members **often lose their homes, farm lands, and equipment. Administering the**

right vaccine in time is critical to the state, national, and global livestock economies!

■ The St. Raphael's Church Building Fund is no more. Until two months ago, the Fund had a balance of $74,000. This past spring, the Church was caught in the eye of a tornado. The concrete foundation was spared, but the roof, windows, and most of the wood structure frame were destroyed. The $74,000 was used to clear the ruins and erect a temporary canvas tent over the foundation. **Times are dire and more bad weather is on the way** …. The Diocese was not prepared financially to build a new larger church.

■ Northern Oregon Rescue has been **barely surviving** on donations from those rescued and a small annual allocation from three County Boards of Commissioners. When we've needed to maintain or replace our rescue gear, **our volunteers have dug deep into their own pockets to cover the costs**. It's no wonder our volunteers are **failing to show up** for rescue calls. No other organization provides **free** rescue services. **The costs of driving up mountains, diving into streams, and leasing a satellite field telephone to call the medevac helicopter for airlifts are straining our meager finances!**

■ If the second largest federally recognized Tribe in the United States cannot find the needed funding to reduce early deaths and keep family members from leaving the reservation, **something is wrong with our country's priorities!** For the past five years, Tribal nations have seen their federal funding reduced by 15% annually. Yes, you're reading this correctly—across America **we've lost 75% of**

our funding base! How can this be true? Just check the Internet for the **ongoing hacking away at funds earmarked for Tribal nations**. When Congress cuts social services programs across the board, this includes monies that would have been allocated to Tribal nations. We're not seeking a handout—just an extended hand to help us lift ourselves up. Our Tribe has no Family Resource Director in any of the three states the reservation covers. **Without the funds to create these positions, Tribal families will continue to disappear at record levels!**

- The **Center's ongoing financial struggle** is no secret. We've been written up by the news media every year in their articles about the embarrassingly low funds available for senior programs in North Dakota. The Mercury River Senior Center is always at the top of the list for highest service population, **highest number of senior users, highest number of disabled senior users, highest number of ADA-related violations, … and lowest number of dollars allocated per senior!**

- The San Juan Housing Authority is only **$100,000 away from fulfilling a 15-year dream** of having public housing units look respectable on the outside. **Block after block of muddy dirt** needs to be covered with grass. Sidewalks are begging to be skirted with flowers that grow year after year. **Children eagerly await the day they can play ball and other outdoor games in their yards**. Money on the island is scarce. Federal funding is limited to the basics and that does not include something as frivolous as landscaping for low-income Puerto Rican families.

■ **Red River Parish is broke!** Yes, that's right, we're so poor we've lost our tax base and we can't seem to get it back. Louisiana is in dire straits because of Hurricanes Katrina and Rita. Scarce funding has been earmarked for the coastal area; this leaves regions farther north like Red River Parish to look for external funding on its own. With no new businesses or convention bookings, there does not seem to be an internal answer to our dilemma.

How Much Is Too Much?

You already know what I'm going to write. Use all of the space allotted by the funder to write about your need. If you are writing a government grant application and the entire narrative section is limited to 25 double-spaced pages, then make sure you have written at least one typed page for every five points assigned to the needs statement. If you're writing a letter proposal or another short format (corporate or foundation), use at least one-fifth of your total pages to write the needs statement.

Chapter 7
The Proposed Program:
Telling About Its Purpose and Place in Your Organization

In this section of your grant proposal narrative, you write about the purpose of your proposed program and how it fits into your organization's overall service structure. It's a very brief section consisting of short paragraphs, one for each "get to it" point.

I always write these brief sentences before I start writing about the program design (goals, objectives, strategies, timelines, and benefits). I'll cover these components in the next chapter.

Elements of a Winning Proposed Program Section:
1. Write Direct and to the Point About the Proposed Program.
2. State How the Proposed Program Fits into Your Organization's Mission.
3. Tell Funders Whether the Proposed Program Is New or an Expansion.

1. Write Direct and to the Point About the Proposed Program

A few chapters back, you learned to write this statement: "The purpose of this request is to seek funding for the ABC Project." In this phrase, you'll be writing almost the same statement—but you'll personalize it with specifics. Your details will help grant readers to refocus on why they're reading a funding request from your organization. Remember: the grant reader has read several pages by now and likely forgotten what the grant will actually fund and who will benefit. It's time to remind the reader about the program you're proposing! Here are some award-winning examples.

- The proposal, when funded, will enable the Wilson Street Animal Shelter to recruit and train 200 additional volunteers for its Mobile Pets on Loan Program. Young children and the elderly will be able to check out a pet on loan for up to three days at no charge. At the end of this time, if the arrangement has been suitable (for children, parents, and seniors), the pet's adoption process will begin. We believe that more abandoned pets will be adopted after they've spent some time with their potential owners.

- United Kingdom Robotics is proposing to research and develop Phase II mobility software for remote-controlled robots. When this proposal is funded, this new software will enable astronauts to direct a device from as far as 5,000 feet away to retrieve soil and water samples. The development of this specialized software will place United

Kingdom Robotics on the world map for software innovations that support advanced space explorations.

- Maritime Restorations will use your financial investment to purchase, transport, and restore the 200-year-old freighter, Batavia II, which is now stored on the Island of Fiji. This ship closes the last known link for the Dutch line of freighters that were lost at sea during the 1800s. Once restored, the ship's historical value will be one hundredfold.

- Days End Respite is proposing to create a daytime care program for individuals of all ages suffering from dementia. This program will be the first in our community. It will enable 50 persons to receive assisted care services and participate in group enrichment activities.

- This proposal from Mama Mia Productions, when funded, will enable our performing group to travel to New Zealand for 45 days, where we will present 20 charitable performances (free of charge) at state-operated orphanages for older children.

- Senate Page Training, Inc. is proposing to develop a new 26-week training program for potential U.S. Senate pages. These coveted positions are difficult to obtain. Your funding will enable 20 potential candidates to receive six months of pre-application training.

- Nana's Lemonade Stand is proposing to train nonprofits in 30 states to start and maintain a Nana's so they can raise funds locally to support further research on pediatric neuroblastoma.

- The Montgomery YWCA is proposing to develop a 65+ Women's Fitness Program to encourage older women to join and enjoy our facility. With your generous funding support, Montgomery women will improve the quality of their lives. And, who knows? They just might live longer too!

- The Charleston NRA Youth Club is proposing a firearms education program for pre-teens and teens—the people most likely to be involved in unintentional fatal injuries when they find their parents' firearms around the house. Your financial support will reduce firearms fatalities.

- The Tennessee Coin Collectors Association is proposing to develop a public outreach and awareness program for people who collect historical coins. With your funding support, rare and valuable coins will be restored and displayed in Tennessee museums, rather than being discarded or sold on the open market.

- This proposal invites the ZYX Foundation to become a stakeholder in the Nebraska League of Cities and Towns new professional development initiative. Your support will enable newly elected officials from every town to attend the new Elected Officials 101 three-hour course, scheduled to be offered in each region three times over the next 12 months.

- The Pierre Medical Center is proposing to purchase the newest MRI scanner available to accommodate overweight and claustrophobic patients of all ages. Once purchased, this radiological scanning equipment will be accessible to patients statewide. Your partnership can benefit thousands of patients who have not fared well or who have avoided the earlier models of MRI scanners.

- This proposal from Serenity Village seeks your support in establishing a new wing for long-term residents. Grant funding will enable us to build a 4,000-square-foot apartment-like wing to accommodate men and women who need longer residential care plans in order to fully recover from substance abuse.

- The Concord Little League is proposing to transport its entire team of 18 players to the New York Yankees spring training camp in Tampa, Florida. Your support for this educational and motivational trip will enable our players to be mentored by a world-famous Major League Baseball player for eight weeks during actual camp games open to the public.

- It's Alive, when funded, will enable pre-school age youth to be introduced to anatomy and physiology. This mobile science lab will travel throughout six counties in the Appalachian Mountains of northern Kentucky where curious young children will be able to have hands-on instruction in animal and human anatomy and physiology.

2. State How the Proposed Program Fits into Your Organization's Mission

- The purpose of the Mobile Pets on Loan Program is to provide an opportunity for potential pet owners to spend quality time with an abandoned animal in hope that they will adopt the pet permanently. This proposed program aligns with the Shelter's mission, which is to place abandoned animals in relationships that are well suited to their needs and to the needs of their future owners.

- United Kingdom Robotics' mission statement encompasses our global direction: To become the world leader in mobility software and maintain that position indefinitely because of our commitment to the research and development of quality products. The proposal to advance to the Phase II research stage aligns with our mission.

- The mission of Maritime Restorations is to locate fragile ships and restore them to their original condition so that the public may enjoy the craftsmanship and history of these precious vessels. The plans to restore the Batavia II align with our mission.

- The Board of Directors envisioned that Days End Respite would be a service to enable those who care for individuals diagnosed with dementia in their homes to take a break—no matter how long. The proposal to begin offering daytime respite services will allow our organization to begin fulfilling its mission.

- The mission statement for Mama Mia Productions is to provide quality-driven and interactive public performances in unexplored venues worldwide. The trip to New Zealand will be our first; however, it will be our fifth tour abroad since 2000. The proposed venue adds yet another achievement for Mama Mia Productions toward fulfilling its mission.

- Senate Page Training, Inc.'s mission is to provide highly skilled, well-trained candidates for U.S. Senate page positions. Our mission was developed in agreement with six former and six current U.S. Senators who made page appointments for multiple terms in office. This proposal aligns with our purpose and direction.

- This proposal supports the Nana's Lemonade Stand philosophy to carry on the spirited work begun by Nana Livingston when she created a nonprofit organization to sell her great-grandmother's lemonade recipe to raise money for research on pediatric neuroblastoma. The full mission statement reads: Every parent or grandparent must take a stand on what they believe in when it comes to saving the life of a child. Nana's Lemonade Stand will dedicate its resources and recipes to helping further the research needed to sustain young lives for as long as humanly possible.

- The Montgomery YWCA's mission is to empower women and girls and to eliminate racism. The proposed 65+ Women's Fitness Program will provide one-on-one, self-building fitness instruction—even for women who have doubts about their physical abilities or who have been left disempowered by life circumstances. Fitness is a fit!

- The vision for the Charleston NRA Youth Club is to educate children of gun owners about the dangers of mishandling firearms. The mission of the NRA is to promote the shooting sports among America's youth. The Charleston Branch is fulfilling the mission of the national organization.

- The mission of the Tennessee Coin Collectors Association is to identify rare coins relevant to the state's history, preserve the coins for public education, and build the reputation of Tennessee in becoming the coin-collecting capital of the world! The initiative proposed aligns with our mission.

- The mission of the Nebraska League of Cities and Towns is to represent the collective interests of cities and towns at the State Legislature, provide timely information on important municipal issues, create skill-sharpening workshops, and develop networking opportunities. The Elected Officials 101 course fits into this mission.

- The mission of the Pierre Medical Center is to provide continuously improved health care services to the residents of South Dakota. The acquisition of this valuable equipment (open MRI scanner) will contribute toward fulfilling this mission.

- Serenity Village has a very unique mission—"Live life to the fullest without drug addiction!" The new wing will enable our clinical staff to work with addicts who need longer 24/7 counseling and supervision in order to live their lives to the fullest without drug addiction.

- The mission of the Concord Little League is to provide a venue for youth to develop mobility skills, build camaraderie with their peers, and be introduced to the basics of the sport of baseball. The trip to Tampa allows our young players to take part in more rigorous pre-game workouts, form alliances with Major League Baseball players, and learn how to play the game from a professional viewpoint.

■ The mission for It's Alive is to stimulate interest in the sciences among young children from an early age. The mobile anatomy and physiology lab is one of several planned mobile and interactive events for our organization. We are on a mission to raise the science literacy levels of Kentuckians.

3. Tell Funders Whether the Proposed Program Is New or an Expansion

- The Mobile Pets on Loan Program is a new outreach initiative for the Wilson Street Animal Shelter.

- The mobility software research proposed is an expansion of the Phase I work that was funded by the National Aeronautics and Space Administration.

- Our aggressive pursuit to restore the Batavia II freighter is an expanded vision for Maritime Restorations. We never thought that a retrieval as far away as Fiji would be within our capabilities until we found your Web site and saw your funding priority for historical ship restoration.

- The daytime caretaker refresher service proposed by Days End Respite is a new initiative intended to expand annually as needed by the target population.

- The proposed trip to New Zealand expands upon our program offerings and vision to impact the underprivileged children of the world with lively and spirited interactive stage productions.

- Senate Page Training, Inc. is a new program developed to meet an emerging need for well-qualified U.S. Senate page candidates.

- The proposed expansion to 30 states is an expansion of Nana's original vision.

- The Montgomery YWCA 65+ Women's Fitness Program is a new initiative to attract older women to our facilities.

- The Charleston NRA Youth Club's firearms mishandling prevention initiative is a new program.

- The Tennessee Coin Collectors Association is expanding efforts that started in 2000 to identify and preserve Tennessee's lost currencies and put them on public display.

- The proposed Elected Officials 101 course is a new initiative for the Nebraska League of Cities and Towns.

- The proposed acquisition of the open MRI scanner is an expanded initiative for the Center. Our facility currently has a 10-year-old closed MRI. With funding, both types of MRI scanners will be available to our patients.

- The proposed addition of a wing for longer-term residential care is a new facility improvement initiative for Serenity Village.

- The proposed trip for the Concord Little League will be the first time—ever—that our group has dared to dream of a cross-country field trip and Major League Baseball educational experience.

- It's Alive is proposing a new initiative for its two-year-old nonprofit organization. We're just getting started!

Chapter 8
Goals, Objectives, Strategies, Timelines, and Benefits:
Presenting the Program Design

You've been eager to write about the well-researched solutions to the problems that you presented in the Needs Statement or Problem Statement. Well, this is the chapter you've been patiently waiting to read. It's time to look at some winning perfect phrases that will help you write magnetizing goal statements and measurable objectives, outline activities or strategies and timelines, and describe the immense benefits for your target population—all made possible by the grant funding.

I want to give you a "where we are" comparison. Many workers refer to Wednesday as hump day. In a traditional work schedule of Monday through Friday, Wednesday was the middle day—with two workdays down and two to go. You and I both know that no one works a regular week any more, but we still use the term "hump." This section of the grant proposal narrative is the hump section: you're halfway through the proposal writing adventure. So, let's get you over the writing hump or off the top of the mountain!

Elements of a Winning Program Design Section:

1. Develop Global Goals and Measurable Objectives.
2. State Proven Strategies, Program Timelines, and Benefits for Your Target Population.
3. Show Funders How Your Program Will Work and Make a Difference in Your Community.

1. Develop Global Goals and Measurable Objectives

The official definition of a goal is the end toward which effort is directed. This means that your goals for the funding results should be written in a way that directly communicates where you want your target population to be by the end of the funding period. How does your target population reach the goals you establish for them? In measurable, quantitative, time-bound steps. These steps are labeled in one of the following ways by different types of funders: outcome objectives, measurable objectives, SMART objectives, or benchmarks. (As mentioned in Chapter 1, SMART means specific, measurable, attainable, realistic, and time-bound.) First you write your goal; then you write the measurable steps you are setting to ensure that your goal is met. Here are some of my examples for winning perfect goal and objective phrases.

- **Goal 1:** Provide alcohol and tobacco abuse education programs and academic tutoring for selected middle school students.
  Objective 1a: By the end of Year 1, high-risk, often truant middle school students will have attended 80% or more of the intervention-based after-school sessions.
  Objective 1b: By the end of Year 1, 90% or more of academically challenged middle school students will raise their grade point averages by one point or more and will be promoted to the next grade.
  Objective 1c: By the end of Year 1, 70% or more of middle

school students completing the alcohol and tobacco abuse education components will have no in- or out-of-school suspensions related to drug sales or possession at school or in the community.

- **Primary Goal 1:** To strengthen the grant applicant's internal capacity in the areas of leadership and organizational development.

  SMART Objective 1: Using baseline leadership development assessment results, by the end of Year 3, 90% or more of the community partners trained and/or receiving one-on-one technical assistance will demonstrate increased competencies in areas identified as deficient or weak.

  SMART Objective 2: Using baseline organizational development assessment results, by the end of Year 3, 90% or more of the community partners trained and/or receiving one-on-one technical assistance will demonstrate increased competencies in areas identified as deficient or weak.

  SMART Objective 3: Using baseline program development assessment results, by the end of Year 3, 90% or more of the community partners trained and/or receiving one-on-one technical assistance will demonstrate increased competencies in areas identified as deficient or weak.

  SMART Objective 4: Using baseline community engagement assessment results, by the end of Year 3, 90% or more of the community partners trained and/or receiving one-on-one technical assistance will demonstrate increased competencies in areas identified as deficient or weak.

- **Specific goals of the Southern Injury Prevention Program are:**
  1. To build a strong coalition of diverse safety organizations committed to reducing fire and burn deaths and injuries among children.
  2. To educate volunteers through leadership seminars by providing them with the knowledge and skills they need to teach fire and burn prevention lessons to students and to conduct the Home Safety Survey in residences.
  3. To implement the fire and burn prevention lessons in 10 elementary schools in high-risk neighborhoods.
  4. To educate children about fire safety issues so they can make safer decisions for themselves and others.
  5. To conduct residential walkthroughs in neighborhoods in order to check and install working smoke detectors and other fire prevention devices.

- **Objectives of the Southern Injury Prevention Program are:**
  1. By the end of Year 1, increase the number of homes with properly functioning smoke detectors by 25% or more in the region found to have the highest incidence of fire-related deaths and injury.
  2. By the end of Year 1, increase the number of homes with additional safety devices by 25% or more in order to prevent other burn-related injuries (chemical and electrical).
  3. By the end of Year 1, increase the number of classrooms participating in unintentional injury prevention education by 50% or more in the targeted areas.

Note: In the collection of perfect phrases above, there are five goals that align with the national funder's five goals. There are only three measurable objectives because the funder asked specifically for these three objectives in its guidelines.

■ The primary goal of the Main Street Historic Preservation Program is to restore the 1912 jail and courthouse for community facilities use and visitor appreciation. The objectives of this aggressive effort to save deteriorating publicly owned buildings in the downtown area are:

1. By the end of Year 1, decrease the number of circa 1900 buildings that are scheduled for demolition by 10% or more.

2. By the end of Year 2, increase the number of deteriorating public buildings that are returned to community use by 10% or more.

3. By the end of Year 2, increase the public's interest and participation in historic preservation by 25% or more by creating a Main Street Community Preservation Council and holding public meetings in the restored building.

■ **Goal:** Expand recreational opportunities for residents and others at Mitchell Park.

   Objective 1: Improve the quality of turf on Mitchell Park soccer and ball fields by 100%.

   Objective 2: Provide adequate water delivery for maintenance of 100% of the park's green space, including soccer and ball fields, for the next 10 years.

   Objective 3: Increase restroom capacity to meet 100% of usage demands for the next 10 years.

2. State Proven Strategies, Program Timelines, and Benefits for Your Target Population

When you develop your goals and objectives, you need to provide a lot of detailed information in order to show your rationale for believing that you can achieve your goals and reach your measurable objectives. This rationale is called "proven strategies." Here are some examples.

Proven Strategies

- According to research conducted by the After School Alliance of Support Networks (2006), academic tutoring works best in the after-school setting immediately following the school day. Each weekday, middle school students are introduced to the curriculum topics and assigned homework. Yet, they are still in need of someone to *break it down into their language and show them how to start and complete the assignment.* The **Middle School Intervention Program** (MSIP) will meet three hours per evening from 3 p.m. to 6 p.m. in each middle school's cafeteria. Small group learning circles (6 to 10 students) will be created for each core curricular area. The circles will be led by high school honor roll students. This older peer support approach will meet the younger students' needs to bond with sibling-like youth. While learning competencies are being achieved, friendships will also be formed.

- Using a proven national leadership development model, the Board of Directors, administrators, and program supervisors will participate in **succession planning training** (facilitated by a contracted consulting firm). Succession planning establishes a process for recruiting employees, developing their skills and abilities, and preparing them for advancement, all while retaining them to ensure a return on the organization's training investment. The proposed **service provider technical assistance and training** strategy is based on the grant applicant's successful organizational sustainability model. The model teaches other community-based organizations best practices in four critical areas of organizational sustainability: 1) leadership development, 2) organizational development, 3) program development, and 4) community engagement.

- The **Southern Injury Prevention Program** (SIPP) will expand and enhance a 2005 SAFE KIDS fire prevention initiative, Flame Out, which targeted one city school and distributed 250 smoke detectors. Like the successful Flame Out pilot model, the SIPP will continue to target the major causes of fire-related deaths and injuries for children—lack of fire-prevention knowledge, absence or deficiency of smoke detectors, absence of fire extinguishers, misuse of tobacco products and matches, space heaters, electrical outlets, and toxic and/or caustic chemicals under the sink. The SIPP will expand the Flame Out model to a wider geographic area, greater community participation, more in-depth training and education for community leaders, 20 times the number of targeted schools, and 8 times the number of smoke detectors.

- The **Main Street Historic Preservation Program's** restoration process for the jail and courthouse is driven by a 2006 building assessment conducted by a historic preservation architect recommended by the State Historic Preservation Division. The architect's findings validate that the building has 65 building code violations. The restoration strategies will follow national historic preservation guidelines and reopen the building for community use and public appreciation.

■ According to the National Parks and Recreation Resource Library (2006), the steps involved in developing a community park are:

1. Start with a core of parks and recreation advocates.
2. Hold a public meeting.
3. Educate the community about the need for a public park.
4. Write a clear park mission statement.
5. Demonstrate a need for another park in a small community.
6. Demonstrate community support.

The Township has diligently followed these steps and is ready to move forward to the next phase of the **Evergreen Village Community Park Development Project**—acquiring funds to expand and upgrade the public amenities at Mitchell Park.

Program Timelines

■ The timelines for the **Middle School Intervention Program** are:

1. On notification of funding, convene meeting with middle school administrators and counselors, high school counselors, and truancy officers to orient them to program goals and objectives and to develop student refer-

ral and facilitator selection processes. Start date: Month 1. End date: Month 1.

2. After a list of students at risk of academic failure has been developed, notify and meet with parents to orient them to the program's purpose and obtain signed permission (for participation) and information release forms (for evaluation purposes). Start date: Month 2. End date: Month 3.

3. Implement all after-school components and establish data collection timeframes. Start date: Month 4 (sessions begin). End date: Ongoing (enrollment and data collection).

■ The timelines for the **Targeted Capacity Expansion Project** are:

1. By the end of the first quarter of Year 1, the Succession Planning Training will be scheduled for all partners. This session will be repeated quarterly throughout the three-year grant funding timeframe.

2. By the end of the second quarter of Year 1, the Communications Strategies Training will be scheduled for all partners. This session will be repeated quarterly throughout the three-year grant funding timeframe.

3. By the beginning of the third quarter of Year 1, partnership members will have developed a workplan for implementing the complete project and will have identified content area trainers and consultants and signed contracts for the delivery of services.

■ Timelines for the **Main Street Historic Preservation Program** are:

1. Stabilization—Year 1.
2. Restoration and Rehabilitation—Year 2.
3. Re-inspection of the Restored Building—Year 2.
4. Community Open House—Year 2.
5. Development and Implementation of Public Use Schedule—Year 2.

- **Timetable for implementation**—Full implementation and all construction for the **Evergreen Village Community Park Development Project** will be completed within 120 days from the receipt of full funding and adequate ground thawing. The following tasks will be completed for Mitchell Park:
  - Preparing bid specifications, advertising the bid specifications, and selecting the low bid (Village Board vote).
  - Installing a new well for the irrigation system.
  - Installing an underground irrigation system for water delivery maintenance of ball fields.
  - Remodeling and enlarging restroom facility.
  - Approving final work completion and issuing remainder of contractor's payment.
  - Scheduling community ribbon cutting and region-wide celebration.

Target Population Benefits

- The **Middle School Intervention Program** will benefit middle school students in the following ways:
  1. Increased self-confidence in being able to understand daily classroom lesson content and able to turn in quality homework assignments.
  2. Increased awareness of the link between getting pass-

ing grades and transitioning successfully to high school and to college and the world of work.

3. Increased skills to resist peer pressure, to just say no to alcohol and other drugs.

- Regional service providers will benefit from the **Targeted Capacity Expansion Program** in the following ways:

1. Boards lead organizations to higher levels of community engagement and sustainability and to recognition of youth programming needs.

2. Combined and cost-effective volunteer recruitment efforts and new levels of trust lead to cross-training and sharing volunteers among partners.

3. Recruitment and retention of high-caliber employees leads to organizational sustainability.

4. Ability to build leadership development capacity leads to agencies contributing more effectively to BFS Partnership mission for youth.

5. Territorial attitudes give way to joint grant applications and interagency subcontracting opportunities.

- The **Southern Injury Prevention Program** will benefit the target population in multiple ways. At a minimum, the cost-benefit analysis for the target population recognizes that the value of the life of one child cannot be quantified. Our coalition members believe that the benefits of this program far outweigh the costs. Dedicating less than $1.00 per resident to this project, the measured payback could be realized by reducing fire-related hospitalizations by just one child next year. Last year, the cost exceeded $200,000 for treating a young house-related burn victim admitted to the

Emergency Department and transferred to the Burn Center at the University of North Carolina. When considering the tragedy experienced by the child and family and the quality of life lost, the cost far transcends dollar amounts.

- The **Main Street Historic Preservation Project** will benefit the public in the following ways:

  1. *Public Education Enhancement and Social Services Delivery Facilitation*—**Groups Benefiting:** Five elementary school districts (Arlington, Buckeye, Liberty, Palo Verde, and Ruth Fisher) and clients of the Literacy Council. **Impact:** A minimum of 12 field trips per year will be accommodated by the Main Street Coalition. Approximately 1,000 young students will learn about regional and local history at the restored building. The Council, which has served over 2,000 illiterate adults in the past decade, will grow because its new location will be conducive to pedestrian traffic. It will attract new volunteers (50 additional) to serve new literacy clients (a minimum of 200 annually) attending learning sessions. Further, students living in adjacent neighborhoods will be able to walk by and view the building or visit in small groups.

  2. *Economic and Community Growth*—**Groups Benefiting:** Tourists passing through our town and residents. The town is strategically located along and across multiple interstate and county transportation corridors (I-10 runs through Buckeye, as do U.S. 85 and MC 85). Many drivers seeking a non-expressway route use MC 85—the main downtown artery of Buckeye, Monroe Street. The

town's present population of 20,000 is projected to grow to 250,000 over the next 10 to 15 years. **Impact:** This project has the potential to become a major historical attraction, opening its doors annually to *2,000 incoming visitors* and *20,000-plus residents (new and old)*.

- The **Evergreen Village Community Park Development Project** will provide increased recreational opportunities at Mitchell Park for over 50,000 residents and non-residents.

3. Show Funders How Your Program Will Work and Make a Difference in Your Community

- The **Middle School Intervention Program** will focus on a core group of middle school troublemakers who have demonstrated bad habits in life choices and public behaviors. This 12-month, intensive academic and behavioral intervention model will help these youths correct their lives, sharpen their decision making, and focus on what really counts—grade progression, reduced absenteeism, and protective factors to help them succeed. The initiative will demonstrate that when additional resources are made available to redirect teenagers from fateful behaviors they can change their attitudes and circumstances, enabling them to reach adulthood and give back to their communities. From community service to leadership roles—they can make a future difference!

- The **Targeted Capacity Expansion Program** will eliminate duplication of services and over-funding for over-served populations. At the same time, the community will benefit from the new level of coordination for wraparound services, monthly service provider duplication reduction meetings, and resulting reprogramming efforts. With government funding at an all-time low for social services programs, this initiative—when funded—will result in a long-lasting working partnerships for our region.

- The **Southern Injury Prevention Program**. Tangible and intangible benefits include the community's enthusiastic endorsement of this project, which will ensure continuity of the project in future years; coalition-building, training, and coordination, which allow fire personnel to focus on technical issues; and the cooperation of the school system, which enables this program to reach children and their families. The safety of our children impacts every person in our community, and reducing childhood fire and burn injuries requires cooperation and consensus of all community residents. County organizations are poised to work together for this endeavor. With your help, we will implement an effective fire and burn prevention program in which education and community involvement can significantly impact the lives of all children in this region and their families.

■ The **Main Street Historic Preservation Program** represents the first effort by our town to reclaim its original public buildings, which have been abandoned and deteriorating for 15 years or longer. This is the first of 20 major restorations planned for the downtown area. This project can add critically needed momentum and economic stimulus for the fulfillment of the Master Revitalization Plan for Downtown—an economic and community development vision. Studies on Smart Growth also show that reinvestment in historic areas in and of itself revitalizes and revalues the investments of both public and private sectors in the vicinity.

■ The **Evergreen Village Community Park Development Project** will provide services at Mitchell Park that enhance the quality of life of all park users. The Village has set goals to develop recreation areas to their fullest possible use to benefit residents and visitors from surrounding counties and states. Fully developed, Mitchell Park will offer the following types of recreational opportunities:

Baseball Field   Softball Field   Little League Field
Practice Ball Field   Soccer Fields   Horseshoe Pit
Practice Soccer Field   Tennis Courts   Roller Hockey Court
Small Tot Play Equipment   Playground Equipment
Picnic Pavilions

On completion of its development, Mitchell Park will be a place where the lives of families are enhanced—and that makes for strong communities.

Knowing How Much to Write

By now, you're used to this rule. However, I want to cover the basics of knowing when to stop writing this narrative section. Always read the funder's narrative formatting guidelines. Use the required font, font size, and line spacing, and write up to the maximum page length allowed—for each section in the narrative and for the total narrative. Space allocations rule all sections of grant proposals!

Chapter 9
Management Plan:
Showing Staff Expertise and Connectivity to the Proposed Program

We're heading for the finish line! You can actually stop and take a deep breath!

In this next set of perfect phrases, you'll learn how to write winning statements to present your project staff or key personnel's qualifications for managing and implementing the grant-funded programs. First, you'll write about who specifically (job title and/or name of person if known) is on your management team and how much of their time will be allocated to the grant-funded program. Second, you'll briefly state their qualifications (education and/or experience). Finally, you'll give potential funders a glimpse of each person's specific responsibilities with your organization and/or the grant-funded program.

Elements of a Winning Management Plan Section:

1. Identify the People Who Will Be Involved in the Grant-Funded Program.
2. Demonstrate Their Qualifications and Suitability for Grant-Funded Positions.
3. Provide Funders with an Overview of Their Specific Grant-Related Responsibilities.

1. Identify the People Who Will Be Involved in the Grant-Funded Program

Include names (if known), job titles, and time assigned to the grant-funded activities.

- The Management Plan for the **Spiritual Rejuvenation Center** includes the following key personnel:
  1. Dr. Melissa Weinstein—Program Administrator, 0.5 FTE (full-time equivalent)
  2. Jeffery Phillips—Program Coordinator, 1.0 FTE
  3. Kara Tyler—Rejuvenation Trainer, 1.0 FTE
  4. Program Assistant (to be hired), 1.0 FTE

- The Management Plan for the **Deep Sea Scientists Association** includes the following professionals:
  1. Dr. Gupta Ramada—Executive Director and Principal Investigator, 1.0 FTE
  2. Dr. Mary Beth McCormick—Director of Marine Biology Research, 1.0 FTE

- The **Wing Star Public Television Foundation** management team includes:
  1. Caroline Foxworthy Smith—Foundation Director, 0.25 FTE
  2. Marietta Anderson—Programming Director, 0.5 FTE

- The **Minnesota Division of Toys for Tots** oversight team includes the following dynamic Minnesota National Guard individuals:
  1. Major James Harrison—Division Commander, 1.0 FTE
  2. Staff Sergeant Mark Matthews—Public Information Officer, 1.0 FTE

3. First Lieutenant Hillary Donaldson—Collections Manager, 1.0 FTE

- The **Rainwater Education Coalition** management team includes the following dedicated volunteers:
  1. Mariah Patterson—President and Lead Educator, 0.5 FTE
  2. Jill St. Marie—Vice President and Community Resource Trainer, 0.25 FTE
  3. John Luther—Treasurer and Environmental Activist Coordinator, 0.25 FTE
  4. Henry Lee—Secretary and Legal Advisor, 0.10 FTE

- The **Littleton Home School Association** is proud to present its leadership team:
  1. Dr. Matilda Griswold—Executive Director, 1.0 FTE
  2. Dr. Jefferson Skywalker—Director of Curriculum, 1.0 FTE

- The **Hill County Medical Society** is led by a core group of dedicated physicians:
  1. Dr. Hezekiah Bibbs—President and Executive Director, 1.0 FTE
  2. Dr. Sharon Stallworth—Vice President and Director of Professional Development, 1.0 FTE
  3. Dr. Dillon Dones—Secretary/Treasurer and Fundraising Executive

- **Legal Eagles** was founded and is currently managed by two lawyers:
  1. Joan Worthington—Executive Director, 1.0 FTE
  2. Thomas Stinson—Services Coordinator, 1.0 FTE

- The **Museum of Contemporary Art** has an exemplary management team:
  1. Edward Anderson—Chief Curator, 1.0 FTE
  2. Henry Grayson—Programming Director, 0.75 FTE
  3. Terry Thompson—Development Officer, 1.0 FTE
  4. Jillian Brooks—Director of Volunteer Services, 0.5 FTE

- **Stepping Stones, Inc.** is managed by:
  1. Miriam Hamilton-Carey—Executive Director, 1.0 FTE
  2. Tony Nash—Community Outreach Specialist, 1.0 FTE
  3. Cicely Meriwether—Parent Educator, 0.5 FTE

2. Demonstrate Their Qualifications and Suitability for Grant-Funded Positions

■ The **Spiritual Rejuvenation Center** prides itself on the exemplary qualifications of the staff assigned to the grant-funded activities. Our staff qualifications follow:

1. Dr. Melissa Weinstein is a certified rejuvenation program developer and manager. She has been developing new rejuvenation chapters around the world, as well as managing the national Center office for 20 years. Dr. Weinstein has given numerous lectures on the benefits of the varying programs at local agencies, schools, universities and hospitals. She holds a doctorate degree in Theology and a master's degree in Business Administration. On behalf of the Center, Dr. Weinstein has appeared on national news and talk shows including *20/20*, *Nightline*, and *The View*.

2. Jeffery Phillips has been employed in the rejuvenation field for 15 years. He has planned and coordinated 10 other grant-funded programs, where he demonstrated exemplary implementation skills. Mr. Phillips completed his undergraduate and postgraduate degree in Switzerland, where he studied Philosophy and Transcendental Meditation at the International University in Geneva.

3. Kara Tyler has been a trainer for 30 years. Her training philosophy stems from her 20-year association with the Art of Peaceful Living Institute. Ms. Tyler developed the first 12 step program for peaceful living. She was recognized by the United Nations Commission on Peace and

Unity for her international work with developing countries at war. Ms. Tyler has created over 40 training modules that are in use worldwide.

4. The Program Assistant, yet to be hired, will possess a bachelor's degree and have at least five years experience in a similar position and the ability to manage organizational equipment and records.

■ The **Deep Sea Scientists Association** is led by two highly qualified and world-renowned marine research scientists:

1. Dr. Ramada holds four graduate degrees. Most relevant to this grant proposal is his master's and doctorate degrees in Limnology and Marine Science from the University of Wisconsin—Madison. He has been a principal investigator on federally funded grants from NASA, NIMH, and NOAA.

2. Dr. McCormick holds a postgraduate degree in Atmospheric and Oceanic Sciences from the University of Maryland. She has been involved in deep sea research since the first Cousteau explorations, where she was hired as an assistant to the project team.

Together, Drs. Ramada and McCormick bring a wealth of invaluable experience to the Association's leadership and research initiatives.

■ The **Wing Star Public Television Foundation** is successful because of two dynamic and extremely qualified key leaders:

1. Caroline Foxworthy Smith has been the Foundation Director since 2000. Since her arrival, Caroline has been responsible for increasing the Wing Star Endowment Fund from $250,000 to $4.6 million. She holds certifi-

cates from the Planned Giving Institute and the Diamond Donor School of Philanthropy. Caroline holds a master's degree from Cambridge University.

2. Marietta Anderson has been our Programming Director for five years. Prior to coming to the Wing Star PBS affiliate, she held similar positions with five public television affiliates in both urban and rural broadcast markets. Marietta attended Brownstone Community College and has an associate's degree in Broadcast Programming.

■ The **Minnesota Division of Toys for Tots** operates a cost-effective, military-style command center for the state's year-around toy collection process. Leading the Command Post are a core group of highly dedicated Minnesota National Guard members:

1. Major James Harrison has been a Division Commander for 10 years. He has been involved in the Toys for Tots initiative for 25 years, joining the Command Post one year after signing up for the Minnesota National Guard. He has led the Division to first place for the number of toys collected annually. In 2004, he received national recognition from the Commander-in-Chief at a Washington, DC ceremony.

2. Staff Sergeant Mark Matthews was assigned to his current position of Public Information Officer in 2005. Prior to that time, he was responsible for authoring and managing *Today's Guard*, which is distributed to 9,000 Minnesota National Guard members. In his current position, Matthews also handles day-to-day communications between the Guard and the civilian media outlets.

3. First Lieutenant Hillary Donaldson joined this Division earlier this year. She comes to Toys for Tots with five years of experience as a volunteer coordinator for Guard spouses. Donaldson also worked in community outreach for 10 years prior to joining the Guard.

- The **Rainwater Education Coalition's** key personnel are:

1. Mariah Patterson, our President and Lead Educator, has been with the Coalition since its founding in 1995. After working 20 years for the U.S. Environmental Protection Agency, Mariah started an educational group to understand the benefits and hazards of preserving rainwater for potable use in American households. She holds a graduate degree in Environmental Sciences from Washington State University.

2. Jill St. Marie, our Vice President and Community Resource Trainer, comes to the Coalition with seven years of experience working in the South American rainforests with the U.S. Peace Corps. She holds degrees in Botany and Environmental Sciences from the University of Centralia Americana in Belize.

3. John Luther, our Treasurer and Environmental Activist Coordinator, comes to us from a 10-year term as Lead Activist for Save Our Forests, the internationally renowned group that stopped tree harvesting in the British Columbia coastal areas. He has helped raise $6 million for the Coalition in two years.

4. Henry Lee, Secretary and Legal Advisor, graduated from Cooley School of Law in Michigan 20 years ago, where he founded Cooley's Pro Bono Environmental

Preservation Legal Unit. Attorney Lee has been with our organization for five years and has proved invaluable in helping to plead cases and arrange bail for our volunteer demonstrators.

- Management team members of the **Littleton Home School Association** are long-time educators and change makers:

  1. Our Executive Director, Dr. Matilda Griswold, served as the state Superintendent of Education for 15 years under Governor Edwin Wise. She was appointed to the Association last year. She holds graduate and postgraduate degrees in Educational Administration. Dr. Griswold taught in the public school system for 20 years and home-schooled her six children prior to entering the workforce.

  2. Dr. Jefferson Skywalker was appointed Director of Curriculum in 1999. He is solely responsible for creating the state-approved home school learning modules. Dr. Skywalker was the Dean of Education at Native University prior to coming to the Association. He holds degrees in Education and Psychology.

- These are **Hill County Medical Society's** leaders:

  1. Dr. Hezekiah Bibbs was elected President in 2000 and named Executive Director in 2006. He retired from 30 years in private practice in facial reconstruction, where he managed a multi-million dollar LLC.

  2. Dr. Sharon Stallworth was elected Vice President in 2000 and named Director of Professional Development in 2001. She came to the Society from the Orange County Medical Society, where she single-handedly increased

membership by 400% in three years. Dr. Stallworth also developed the 30-hour Practitioner's Edge professional development model that was recently accredited by the U.S. Medical Society.

3. Dr. Dillon Dones was elected Secretary/Treasurer in 2004 and named Fundraising Executive in 2006. He comes to the Society with 10 years of donor relations experience with the U.S. Fundraising Professionals Association. Dr. Dones has been able to use his medical profession connections as retired Chief of Staff from Boston Medical Center to create revenue streams in excess of $5 million per year for his past employer and now for the Society.

- **Legal Eagles** is successful because of:

1. Joan Worthington, J.D., was appointed Executive Director in 1985. During her 20-plus years with the organization, she has created multiple legal education outreach programs in the District's low-income and crime-ridden neighborhoods. Attorney Worthington is a graduate of George Washington University School of Law. In 2004, she was awarded the coveted Eagle award by the District Bar Association.

2. Thomas Stinson, the Services Coordinator, has been a certified legal assistant for 20 years. He formerly worked as a legal researcher for Supreme Court Justice Sandra Elizabeth Cummings. Mr. Stinson graduated from Allegany Community College with a certificate as Legal Assistant. He also attended St. Louis University and graduated from Carnegie Mellon University with a

degree in Legal Systems. Mr. Stinson has completed 1.5 years of law school courses in an online study program.

- Key management team members at the **Museum of Contemporary Art** are:

1. Chief Curator Edward Anderson came to the Museum in 1992 after 20 years with the Smithsonian Institute. He earned a Master's of Liberal Studies with Museum Emphasis from the University of Oklahoma's College of Liberal Studies in 1969.

2. Programming Director, Henry Grayson, found his way to the Museum in 1999, when he was assigned by WKBT-TV to cover the Museum's 40th Anniversary Celebration. In talking with staff, board members, and visitors, Mr. Grayson developed an interest in our operations. Since joining our staff, he has created new and innovative community programming, which has resulted in an increase in group visits from new types of emerging art lovers.

3. Development Officer, Terry Thompson, came to the Museum from the Albuquerque International Balloon Museum. Ms. Thompson helped the Executive Director raise $2.4 million to build a new facility. Since 2003, she has taken the Museum's endowment fund from $100,000 to $6.7 million. She has a graduate degree in Nonprofit Management from the University of Indiana.

4. Director of Volunteer Services, Jillian Brooks, has been at the Museum since January of this year. Prior to that, she held a similar position with the United Way of Cove Station, Kentucky. Ms. Brooks holds a bachelor's degree

in Human Services Management and is enrolled in the Museum Administration master's program at Finlay State University.

- **Stepping Stones, Inc.** has a dynamic and dedicated management team:

1. Miriam Hamilton-Carey, our Executive Director, created the Stepping Stones concept five years ago when she realized that not all young girls fit into the traditional "Girls Club" groups. Her insightfulness evolved into a statewide adolescent teen development program for inner-city girls. Under her leadership, the program has grown to 24 chapters and enrolled 457 young women.

2. Tony Nash, our Community Outreach Specialist, met the Executive Director at a Youth for Christ rally in 2000 and came on board when Ms. Hamilton-Carey opened the first Stepping Stones chapter. Mr. Nash graduated from the University of Phoenix with a degree in Business Management. He earned his master's degree in Mass Communications from Arizona State University's Walter Cronkite School of Mass Communications.

3. Cicely Meriwether, our Parent Educator, is a single parent who raised three sets of twin girls alone after her husband died suddenly. To support herself, she attended college while the girls were in school. Cicely earned her bachelor's degree in Parent Support Services from Florida State University. She has been with Stepping Stones for two years.

3. Provide Funders with an Overview of Their Specific Grant-Related Responsibilities

If you're requesting program- or project-specific funds, write in *future* tense using "will" to detail the duties of your key personnel. If you're requesting general operating support, write in *present* tense to detail what the key staff person currently does for the grant applicant organization.

- For the **Spiritual Rejuvenation Center** (new program request):
  1. The Program Administrator's grant-related duties will include grant program management oversight, meeting with community partners, supervising all program staff, and reviewing and approving final fiscal and evaluation reports for communication with funders and other investors.
  2. The Program Coordinator's grant-related duties will include coordinating the new program with all other operating chapters and with local, regional, national, and international partners. He will also be responsible for working with the evaluator and stakeholders evaluation team to track the new program's implementation process.
  3. The Rejuvenation Trainer will be responsible for developing and carrying out all training curricula at the Center's headquarters. In addition, this position will oversee the implementation of training modules at chapters worldwide and participate in the selection of trainers and ongoing monitoring and evaluation.

4. The Program Assistant will be hired after the grant has been awarded. The individual selected for this position will be responsible for assisting the administrative staff and trainer in their day-to-day project implementation needs.

■ For the **Deep Sea Scientists Association** (new program request):

1. The Executive Director and Principal Investigator will be responsible for developing and monitoring all Association contracts with individual non-member scientific exploration teams. This position will also plan the NOAA Conference for Deep Sea Scientists, maintain the Association's federal partnerships, and be responsible for all grant management tasks.

2. The Director of Marine Biology Research will be responsible for validating the data collected and reported by members of the research team and publishing their findings in *Deep Sea Today*, the Association's international research journal. On occasion, the Director will travel to exploration sites and provide technical assistance relative to validating findings and issuing media reports on irregular findings.

■ For the **Wing Star Public Television Foundation** (general operating request):

1. The Foundation Director is responsible for developing the annual fundraising plan, carrying out action steps approved by the Board of Directors, managing grants, and working with Wing Star University faculty and staff to increase payroll deduction commitments to the Foundation.

2. The Programming Director is responsible for managing the station's daily programming links to PBS. In addition, this person assists with Foundation on-air phonathons and other special fundraising events that are broadcast.

- For the **Minnesota Division of Toys for Tots** (capacity-building request):

1. The Division Commander is responsible for overseeing all Toys for Tots operations and managing grants. This person requires the highest level of management and communications skills. The Commander must be able to convey sensitive operations information to both his superiors and his subordinates. In addition, this person is required to lead in carrying out military orders and investigating civilian complaints.

2. The Public Information Officer must be able to address all media inquiries, write error-free press releases, and represent the Command Post and the Minnesota National Guard in all public meetings and ceremonial appearances. At no time will the Division receive negative publicity under the Public Information Officer's watch.

3. The Collections Manager is responsible for coordinating statewide collection processes and maintaining a daily count of incoming toys and total toys in inventory. In the event that a manufacturer recalls a toy, the Collections Manager must personally oversee the removal of dangerous toys from each of the state's 20 toy warehouses. The Collections Manager must work

closely with the Public Information Officer to help publicize toy shortages and garner civilian media support in publicizing the toy drive's needs.

- For the **Rainwater Education Coalition** (capacity-building request):
  1. The Lead Educator is responsible for researching relevant topics, collecting critical statistics, and reviewing emerging ecological practices worldwide. This person must be able to communicate effectively to media groups and testify before the World Rainwater Alliance and the U.S. Congress when requested. Grant management tasks are also included in this person's responsibilities.
  2. The Community Resource Trainer must have extensive knowledge of environmental agencies, services, and programs beneficial to training others about community resources. This person must keep abreast of all global issues related to rainwater contaminants and how to remove them safely.
  3. The Environmental Activist Coordinator is responsible for recruiting demonstrators, training them in Coalition public demonstration protocol, and providing them with information on handling protester arrests. The Coordinator must be willing to follow the policies and philosophy for the Peaceful Protesting Alliance, of which the Rainwater Education Coalition is a member.
  4. The Legal Advisor functions as a key member of the management team. This person must provide strong leadership, exercise prudent judgment, and have solid

business acumen in order to partner effectively with other rainwater education groups. The Legal Advisor must be able to anticipate issues and trends proactively and keep the management team fully advised.

- For the **Littleton Home School Association** (capacity-building request):

1. The Executive Director must be able to demonstrate commitment to participatory management and team leadership models, with an ability to effectively deal with crisis situations. This person must also be able to empower staff, through building ownership and accountability of decisions. The Executive Director must also be able to interact effectively and collaborate with various stakeholders, including parents and auxiliary entities, and manage all grant administration tasks.

2. The Director of Curriculum must work with principals, directors, teachers, and subject matter specialists in developing curriculum consistent with Association philosophy and goals. This person also coordinates and evaluates the curricula and instructional programs and makes appropriate recommendations for change and/or modification.

- For the **Hill County Medical Society** (program-expansion request):

1. The Executive Director is responsible for working with relevant committees, state leaders, the House of Delegates, and the Board of Directors as needed. This person must also help write and edit Society policies and keep membership informed on legislative and reg-

ulatory developments. The Executive Director also assists members by providing information and referral regarding key issues.

2. The Director of Professional Development is responsible for monitoring compliance with state Continuing Medical Education requirements and maintaining departmental feedback on programs recommended for attendance. This person also coordinates all non-medical professional training, such as diversity and sexual harassment awareness.

3. The Fundraising Executive is responsible for developing and maintaining the Society's alumni directory, either hard copy or electronic. This person also develops an electronic newsletter notification system for alumni, using the firm's extranet capabilities. Grant management tasks are also a part of this person's responsibilities.

- For **Legal Eagles** (operating-support request):

1. The Executive Director is responsible for overseeing all of the Center's activities to ensure operational and programmatic effectiveness, including grant management. The Executive Director also oversees all personnel in hiring, staff orientation, and staff development and the Center's administrative and financial management systems, including the annual budget planning process and the annual audit, and office procedures and systems.

2. The Services Coordinator is responsible for identifying all needed pro bono services for clients and bringing in legal experts to fulfill clients' needs. In addition, the Services Coordinator is responsible for monitoring the

delivery of services and the outcomes for clients receiving free legal aid. Where legal precedents will be set, the Services Coordinator must work closely with the Judicial Committee at the Center to determine the best approach to take for the client's defense.

- For the **Museum of Contemporary Art** (operating-support request):
  1. The Chief Curator is responsible for choosing and acquiring the pieces of art to be shown in a museum, both for permanent display and for special temporary exhibitions. This person also decides how the pieces should be displayed and the order in which they appear.
  2. The Programming Director works closely with the Chief Curator to design educational programs, tours, workshops, and lectures to publicize collections.
  3. The Development Officer is responsible for soliciting grant awards, securing donations of artwork from collectors, and getting business firms to fund special exhibitions. In addition, this person plans special fundraising events, such as high-end formal dinners, annual exhibit day events, and other duties as assigned by the Board of Directors.
  4. The Director of Volunteer Services is responsible for designing, planning, and directing the Museum's volunteer program to augment the services of the regular staff. This person also oversees the recruiting, interviewing, hiring, training, and scheduling of volunteer workers.

- For **Stepping Stones, Inc.** (program-expansion request):
  1. The Executive Director is responsible for cultivating donors, coordinating volunteers, managing grants, managing and facilitating fundraising events, and administering all scholarship and grant programs under the direction of the Board of Directors.
  2. The Community Outreach Specialist is responsible for recruiting eligible girls for enrollment into local chapters. In addition, this person is responsible for conveying the mission and purpose of our programs to community service organizations that have the potential to make annual contributions.
  3. The Parent Educator is responsible for recruiting parents of enrolled girls and helping them form peer–parent support groups. The Parent Educator must also create training modules related to positive parenting, passive disciplining, understanding adolescent development, and recognizing signs that a daughter is in trouble.

How Much Do You Include in the Proposal Narrative?

The amount of information that you include in your proposal narrative depends on the space allocation and peer review points designated by the funding agency. If you don't have sufficient room, simply write a sentence or two about each member of the management team and attach their one-paragraph biographies for further review by the grant reader.

Chapter 10
Evaluation Plan:
Validating Your Solution to the Problem

I used to cringe when it was time to write the Evaluation Plan. However, I overcame the fear of writing this accountability narrative by just practicing—over and over. Some evaluation narratives are simple and others are more complex. In this chapter, I'm giving you some perfect phrases for simple and complex evaluation plans.

Elements of a Winning Evaluation Plan Section:
1. Identify the People Who Will Conduct the Evaluation.
2. Reiterate the Measurable Objectives and State How They Will Be Evaluated.
3. Provide Funders with Your Data Collection and Reporting Process.

1. Identify the People Who Will Conduct the Evaluation

- **For a Performing Arts Musical Group:**
  The Board of Directors will take responsibility for developing a team of stakeholders (board members, volunteers, and long-time patrons) to carry out the Evaluation Plan.

- **For a Hazardous Materials Training Center Construction Project:**
  The staff of the Hazardous Materials Center will be responsible for designing the evaluation tools and preparing evaluation reports. However, a team of facility stakeholders will be convened to evaluate the overall performance of the HMTC upon completion of the expansion construction. These stakeholders will be trainees from Michigan and elsewhere in the nation. They will be asked to rate each of the project's objectives and give feedback on expanded programming.

- **For an Organization with a National Affiliate:**
  On the national level, the U.S. Safety Council Research Director will undertake the tasks for the national and local evaluations. This individual has been conducting evaluations for the past 20 years and has extensive experience in all evaluation methodologies.

- **For a Large Urban School District:**
  The District will contract with Dr. Peter Edwards. He has conducted past evaluations for the MDUSD SS/HS Partnership Initiative. Dr. Edwards earned his Ph.D. in Community Education and Administration from the

University of Florida. He has agreed to contract with the District for the five-year funding period.

■ **For a Nonprofit Developing a Revenue-Generating Retail Outlet:**

The evaluation will be conducted by two separate stakeholder groups. The first evaluation group will be the women trained in the patchwork quilt making program whose merchandise will be for sale at the expanded retail outlet. The second evaluation group will consist of local economic development staff, banking loan officers, and the New Rochelle Incubator management team.

■ **For a Community-Based Mentoring Program:**

The evaluation will be conducted by a contracted third-party consultant. The grant applicant will work with local universities to identify faculty members with expertise in the program area.

■ **For a Fire Safety and Education Program:**

The evaluation will be conducted onsite at each of the targeted elementary schools. Using a stakeholder approach, teachers, administrators, students, and their parents will be asked to provide feedback on the impact of the program.

■ **For a Community Players Theatrical Group:**

The evaluation process will be conducted by the core group of volunteers who serve as ushers, ticket takers, and in other roles. Each of the volunteers (10) has been with the Community Players for five or more years and can objectively collect patron feedback, assess their interest in the current schedule of performances, and provide valuable information to our Board of Directors.

■ **For an Employment and Training Program:**
Dr. Barbara Billings, a biracial African American and Native American grant writing consultant and program evaluator, will work with I Can Project consultants to develop evaluation tools, monitor the data collection process, interpret the data, and prepare findings reports for all stakeholders.

■ **For a Family Preservation Program:**
The Lead FCPA Intensive Family Preservation Program Specialist will be responsible for collecting the data to compile the Annual Summary of Participants and Outcome. The LCYF-FPP Monitoring Unit and the District LCYF Grants Administrator will be responsible for the Intensive Family Preservation performance assessment.

■ **For a Teen Health and Diversity Program:**
The grant applicant will contract with Everett, Billings, and Williamson (EBW), an evaluation firm located 50 miles from our program implementation site. EBW has agreed to design the data collection tools and make monthly site visits to meet with youths, program staff, and community agencies. EBW has evaluated other programs funded by the Vermont United Way and is familiar with the Logic Model process and its reporting requirements.

■ **For a Multi-Service Center Renovation Project:**
The evaluation will be conducted by the West Memphis Community College economic development and public health services faculties. They are most familiar with the impact area and the target population for the new facility.

2. Reiterate the Measurable Objectives and State How They Will Be Evaluated

- **For a Performing Arts Musical Group:**

  Objective 1a: Raise 100% of the funds needed to present 16 planned performances.

  Measurement: Number of new financial supporters and amount of funds received.

  Objective 2a: Increase media exposure by 50% or more through radio, newspaper, brochure, and direct mail advertising.

  Measurement: Comparison of paid attendance counts in 2004–2005 performance period with counts from previous performance periods.

  Objective 3a: Increase performances for school-age audiences by 25% or more and work to align accompanying music history lecture with the Pennsylvania Department of Education's Academic Standards for Arts and Humanities.

  Measurement: Number of lectures and accompanying performances for school-age children and feedback from students and teachers.

  Objective 4a: Increase awareness of performances by 50% or more and align potential sponsorships with new partners.

  Measurement: Number of agreements and number of underwritten performances.

- **For a Hazardous Materials Training Center Construction Project:**

  Objective: Collect 100% of the $300,000 needed to start

construction from the private sector, including previous contributors to the HMTC as well as new partners.

Measurement: Log of funding sources approached, funds received, including source, date received, and amount received. Written notice to all funders when 100% of funds are on deposit.

Objective: Expand the course offerings and available classes by 50% or more over the previous year's capacity.

Measurement: Comparison report for number of courses offered prior to expansion and number of courses offered in the previous year's course catalog.

- **For an Organization with a National Affiliate:**

Objective: Community partners experience an increase of 30% or more in their knowledge of homeland security issues, how they can help strengthen public safety, and their role in supporting county-based People's Corps Councils.

Measurement: Pre- and post-program Homeland Security Awareness Surveys.

Objective: Safe People Foundation experiences an increase of 30% or more in annual financial support toward the Special Volunteer Program goals.

Measurement: Amount of cash contributions; value of in-kind contributions; percentage of total funds from grants; and pre- and post-program surveys of council leadership, training, and volunteer organizing strengths and weaknesses.

Objective: People's Corps Councils experience an increase of 30% or more in special volunteers.

Measurement: Baseline survey of current volunteer pool in each county and ongoing tracking of numbers of new special volunteers in each county.

Objective: People's Corps Councils experience a 25% or more increase in volunteers with diverse heritage and cultural backgrounds.

Measurement: Baseline survey of current volunteer pool composition. Voluntary information collected on volunteer intake form.

■ **For a Large Urban School District:**

Performance Indicator 1.1.1: Annually update 30% of the security devices in the District's buildings.

Measurement: Number of devices updated and number of buildings with devices.

Performance Indicator 1.1.2: Annually train 30% of staff in security and crisis procedures.

Measurement: Number of staff trained.

Performance Indicator 1.1.3: Annually decrease by 30% opportunities for students to bring weapons and hard drugs onto the school campus.

Measurement: Number of random backpack and locker searches and number of students who are found to have weapons and hard drugs on the school campus.

■ **For a Nonprofit Developing a Revenue-Generating Retail Outlet:**

Measurable Objectives:

1. Expand Center's staffing by 50% or more.
2. Expand Center's operating hours by 40%.

3. Increase materials and equipment inventory by 50%.
4. Increase outlet space by 500%.
5. Increase outlet visibility by 50% or more.
6. Increase outlet retail sales by 100%.

Measurements Tracked:

1. Number of new staff hired compared to baseline staff levels.
2. Number of operating hours per week compared to baseline hours.
3. Amount of materials and equipment in inventory compared to baseline levels.
4. Amount of square footage in new facility compared to baseline square footage.
5. Number of customers walking through the door compared to baseline count.
6. Amount of annual retail sales compared to baseline revenues.

- **For a Community-Based Mentoring Program:**

Objective 1a: By the end of the second grading period, 70% or more of at-risk youth enrolled in the program will show an improvement in academic performance by raising a failing grade by one grade level.

Measurement: Number of students who previously failed who pass subject area examinations.

Objective 1b: By the end of the second semester, 70% or more of at-risk youth enrolled in the program will show an increase in knowledge about peer coping and social skills and ability to apply them.

Measurement: Pre- and post-program surveys comparing

the number of learning competencies for each student in the areas of peer coping and social skills.

Objective 1c: By the end of the second semester, 50% or more of at-risk youth enrolled in the program will perceive the use of alcohol, tobacco, and other drugs as life-threatening, habitual, and the beginning of long-term court involvement.

Measurement: Pre- and post-program surveys comparisons of the number of individual risk factors identified by students.

Objective 1d: By the end of the second semester, 50% or more of at-risk youth enrolled in the program will perceive carrying and using firearms as a fatal action.

Measurement: Pre- and post-program surveys of the number of students demonstrating their knowledge of firearm danger and consequences.

Objective 2a: By the end of the first semester, 90% or more of at-risk youth enrolled in the program will identify, plan, and become involved in a community service project.

Measurement: Number of students completing their community service projects.

■ **For a Fire Safety and Education Program:**

Objective 1: Increase child injury prevention knowledge among Latinos by 25% or more.

Measurement: Pre- and post-program surveys of parents and students on child injury prevention competencies.

Objective 2: Expand school-based fire and life safety public education activities by 25% or more.

Measurement: Number of students enrolled in Spanish fire and life safety learning modules vs. baseline numbers.

Objective 3: Increase the "Familias Viajando A Seguridad" Program sites by 100% in the second six months of the FEMA funding year.

Measurement: Number of schools participating and number of classrooms participating,

Objective 4: Offer bilingual injury prevention curriculum to at least 40% or more of the county's more than two dozen communities.

Measurement: Number of additional communities requesting copies of curriculum modules and train-the-trainer training.

Objective 5: Reduce unintentional fire and water injuries among preschool-age Latino children by 25% or more.

Measurement: Number of reported fire and water injuries among target population in comparison with baseline numbers.

■ **For a Community Players Theatrical Group:**
Objective: To increase ticket sales for our performances by 90% over the next two performance seasons.
Measurement: Number of tickets sold.

■ **For an Employment and Training Program:**
Objective 1: 75% of participants will retain their jobs in unsubsidized employment after 6, 9, and 12 months.

Objective 2: 60% of participants will seek continued occupational skills training in high-wage trade areas to further their career.

Measurements: Number of participants able to work six months, nine months, and 12 months without an interruption in their employment period.

■ **For a Family Preservation Program:**

Objective 1: 95% of families referred for IFPP service provision will express satisfaction with FCPA's service delivery, as indicated on the Client Satisfaction Survey issued to families at the close of their cases.

Measurement: Number of families enrolled. Number of families referred. Number of families completing the survey. Number of families indicating satisfaction.

Objective 2: 90% of the LCYF Case Managers who received services provided by FCPA during the time period will express satisfaction with FCPA's service delivery.

Measurement: Number of open cases requiring case management communications between FCPA and LCYF. Number of Case Managers taking the survey. Number of Case Managers indicating satisfaction.

■ **For a Teen Diversity Program:**

Objective 1: 90% or more of youths enrolled in the POLI who have been victims of intolerance and hate will gain confidence in their ability to exhibit peaceful and prideful leadership skills among hostile peers and adults.

Measurement: Number of youths responding differently to post-program survey in comparison with pre-propgram survey responses about peace and pride as they relate to leadership skills.

Objective 2: 50% or more of youths enrolled in POLI who have been perpetrators of verbal and physical aggressiveness toward youths who are different from them will acknowledge the need to break generational behavior toward "newcomers, minorities, and other youth who are different because of religious beliefs, sexual orientation, or appearance."

Measurement: Number of youths exhibiting behavioral and perception changes on pre- and post-program surveys.

Objective 3: 60% or more of youth victims and perpetrators will become advocates for teen tolerance and diversity in the Far West Valley.

Measurement: Number of youths willing to participate in Diversity Day march and picnic and number of youths who actually show up for the events. Number of youths who indicate they are interested in future programs and events to reduce hate and intolerance.

■ **For a Multi-Service Center Renovation Project:**

Objective 1: By the end of 2008, increase by 25% or more the number of initial county service providers committed to becoming paying tenants at the Mississippi Crossroads Community Services site.

Measurement: Number of sub-leases signed initially and number signed in 2008.

Objective 2: By the end of 2008, increase by 50% or more the number of LMI clients traveling to the city of West Memphis for social services and other provider-based needs.

Measurement: Number of low- and moderate-income clients receiving services at new site who did not travel to the city of West Memphis previously to access social services.

Objective 3: By the end of 2008, decrease by 70% or more regional community risk factors related to access barriers, services availability, and fragmented services coordination.

Measurement: Pre- and post-program community needs assessment comparisons.

Objective 4: By the end of 2008, decrease by 25% or more the facilities-related administrative overhead for Mississippi Crossroads tenants by offering shared, low-cost common services.

Measurement: Pre- and post-propgram administrative overhead cost comparisons.

3. Provide Funders with Your Data Collection and Reporting Process

■ **For a Performing Arts Musical Group:**

Interim (at six months) and final (at 12 months) evaluation reports will be prepared and sent to all grantors. The evaluation reports will contain the year-to-date financial report (expenses paid by grant funding from each funder) and progress attainment of the measurable objectives. Letters from patrons will be included in the final report.

■ **For a Hazardous Materials Training Center Construction Project:**

Stakeholders (including funders) will receive quarterly interim reports with qualitative and quantitative data interpretations. At the end of the construction phase, the final pro forma with end dates for deliverables will be included in the third quarter report. The summative report (fourth quarter) will include the data to support the objective for course expansions and a list of all funders supporting the project.

■ **For an Organization with a National Affiliate:**

For the outcome evaluation process, formative and summative evaluation data will be collected and findings will be reported quarterly and annually for the three-year proposed funding timeframe. For the process evaluation, data will be collected twice annually and reported in the same frequency.

■ **For a Large Urban School District:**

Evaluation methods will include anonymous surveys of

participants in various programs or services for the purpose of collecting feedback data and empowering participants. Process data will be collected at monthly site-based advisory team meetings and yearly from all partners. This data will provide insight into supports needed for increased collaboration. Annual statistical data related to rates of violence, attendance, service frequencies, and the rest of the element indicators will be reviewed at the beginning of each school year. Reports will be produced semiannually for formative feedback purposes and annually for summative feedback purposes.

- **For a Nonprofit Developing a Revenue-Generating Retail Outlet:**
Data on the Center's measurements will be collected weekly using revenue tracking logs with breakout reports for high sales days and high sales items. Customers will be asked for their ZIP codes and how they heard about the Center's retail outlet. In addition, the community perception evaluation results will be reported monthly to assess the Center's impact on the city at large. Qualitative and quantitative data will help the Center's Board change its displays, pricing, and advertising to meet and hopefully exceed customer and community satisfaction.

- **For a Community-Based Mentoring Program:**
Reporting Frequency. Data reporting will be formative (quarterly) and summative (end of program).

Stakeholder Involvement. All stakeholders will be involved in the data samplings and reporting. Interim and final evaluation reports will be provided to participant groups in debriefing forums, to Advisory Board members (each program will have an Advisory Board made up of representatives from community partners and the stakeholders group), and to funding agencies.

Data Collection Tools. A pre- and post-program survey will be administered to students from the cohort group and the comparison group at the beginning and end of the school year. The survey will collect information on demographics/family status, school engagement (asking questions such as "How important is it to you to do well in school?" and "Do you have a quiet place to do homework?"), school engagement indicators (such as frequency of truancy, not completing homework, court involvement, use of drugs, carrying weapons, gang involvement, status of siblings [dropout, incarcerated, involved in crime]), risky behaviors (such as lack of supervision and substance abuse), self-concept (anger management, peer pressure, positive role models, and other risk identification questions), current after-school involvement, and other extracurricular involvement (including volunteering, athletics, and school clubs).

- **For a Fire Safety and Education Program:**
  The collected data will be reviewed by a county-wide Fire Safety and Education Committee (members from the 15 metro area fire departments) who will interpret the data and work with our office to compile the results. Interim (quarterly) and final (12 months) reports will be typed and distributed to schools, parents, fire department administrators, and community partners and also uploaded into the FEMA system during the closeout reporting process.

- **For a Community Players Theatrical Group:**
Measures of Success
Comparison Studies: Success will be gauged in terms of audience satisfaction (ratings on a five-point scale) compared with other community theater experiences. Studies will be done over the six-month performance season and reported within 90 days post-season.

Measurement of Production Quality: Audience surveys will be taken at every monthly performance. Though higher overall satisfaction levels will be sought, maintenance of equivalent levels will be considered successful until greater experience with this measurement can be obtained.

Measurement of Improved Actor and Crew Skills: We will conduct random and informal interviews with actors and crews (monthly) for their feedback about the quality of the environment the Community Players Theatrical Group provides them.

Data will be reported at the end of the year. Our findings will be issued to all stakeholder groups.

- **For an Employment and Training Program:**

An ethnostatistical evaluation approach will be used:

1. Culturally sensitive program surveys of participants and employers (collected pre- and post-program and responses compared to measure program's systemic impact on stakeholders).

2. Culturally sensitive case management entry and exit interviews (collected pre- and post-employment readiness data and compared responses to measure participant impact).

3. On-the-job observations by monitors who are of the same ethnicity as the subpopulation (collected pre- and post-employability skills and job acculturation data and compared responses to measure job level satisfaction, career mobility, and job sustainability impact).

Quarterly reports will be uploaded into the E-Fund system for funder review. Final closeout statistics will be uploaded within 30 days of the end of the I Can Project.

■ **For a Family Preservation Program:**

The evaluator will submit copies of the completed surveys with the end-of-the-month reports. LCYF will compile the results of the survey and the results will be shared with FCPA. In addition, an annual survey will be administered to case managers in the second quarter of each contract year. The evaluator will compile the results, which will then be shared with all stakeholders. Additional documentation will include a compilation of monthly outcome measurements tracking the number of unduplicated cases opened and closed during the contract period.

■ **For a Teen Diversity Program:**

The program will be evaluated for qualitative and quantitative outcomes. The reporting frequencies will meet the requirements for both of the potential funders: the state of Vermont and the Vermont United Way. Results of the evaluation findings will also be posted on the grant applicant's Web site so that other small communities can replicate the implementation model.

■ **For a Multi-Service Center Renovation Project:**

The project will be evaluated for its impact on the targeted region. A process evaluation will be conducted on the facilities renovation and tenant leasing. An outcome evaluation will be conducted to determine benefits to the target population. Findings will be interpreted by the contracted third-party evaluator and reports will be compiled for stakeholders to review. This project is not just a renovation initiative; it is a major social experiment to observe how people respond when social services access barriers are eliminated. Will they seek the needed services? Will they improve their economic, physical, and education statuses? These are two key findings that could have a rippling impact on positioning multiple social services under one roof in a centralized location.

How Will You Know How Much to Write?

Adhere to the funder's guidelines for length and narrative content limitations. This is a rule to follow; otherwise, your grant proposal might never be reviewed or funded.

Part Three

Perfect Phrases for the Attachment Documents

Chapter 11
Budget:
Connecting the Proposal Budget to the Program Design and Highlighting Contributions

As a grant writing consultant, I really prefer that my clients read the grant proposal narrative draft and then start fleshing out their budget. Most of the time, I can convince them to develop the budget narrative. The rest of the time, I have to flesh out the numbers myself!

In this chapter, I want to show you how to connect the budget narrative with the program design narrative, help you identify the sources of your in-kind and cash contributions, and give you some perfect phrases for writing about your internal resources and sustainability.

Remember: keep the budget section of your grant proposals factual and always round off your budget numbers to the nearest dollar.

Elements of a Winning Budget Section:

1. Connect the Proposal Budget to Your Program Design Tasks.
2. Include Your Organization's and Its Partners' Cash and in-Kind Contributions.
3. Provide Funders with a Solid Plan for Sustainability.

1. Connect the Proposal Budget to Your Program Design Tasks

■ **Key Tasks for an International Wellness Research Institute** (request to foundation):

1. Mainstream courses will be taught monthly and youth programs will be taught quarterly.
2. Special health courses (e.g., depression, cancer, HIV) will be offered to increase our services in special needs communities. Planning would take place within the first quarter.

Budget Narrative

Personnel – $60,000

$45,000 – Training Coordinator (1) @1.0 FTE. This individual will supervise all training-related tasks. Responsibilities include contracting with course topic experts, advertising the training programs, selecting training sites, monitoring registration, and monitoring and evaluating training content.

$25,000 – Administrative Assistant (1) @ 1.0 FTE. This individual will provide clerical support to the Training Coordinator.

Fringe Benefits – $20,000

The fringe benefits are calculated at 30% of the two salaries. Health insurance is $15,000 annually, the required employer FICA match of 7.65% is $1,530, workers' compensation at 3.6% is $720, and term life insurance at 13.75% is $2,750.

Office and Training Operations – $48,000

The projected expenditures include supplies, printing, telephone, Internet connection, Web site maintenance, postage, and rented offices and meeting space. The rented space accounts for 70% or $33,600 annually. The remaining items have been estimated at a cost of $1,200 per month, $14,400.

Contractual Agreements – $36,000

This line item is to support the training fees of facilitators who will be contracted to deliver courses on general health and wellness, adolescent development processes, HIV prevention, cancer awareness education, signs of depression, and holistic living. Trainings will cost an average of $3,000 per month.

Total Budget Request: $164,000.

- **Key Tasks for Post-Secondary Capacity-Building Project** (request to foundation):
  1. Organizational capacity-building workshops.
  2. Identification, compilation, and dissemination of print/electronic resources.
  3. Creation of online courses and pedagogical materials.

Budget Narrative

Summer Training and Professional Development Workshops: These weeklong workshops will have two primary purposes. The first is to train university staff members in the use of information technology, including Web authoring techniques, to the point that they will be able to use these technologies to develop and mount pedagogical and cultural materials on their individual campus Web sites and also be able to share these skills with Center students, many of whom come to their campuses significantly behind their mainstream peers in experience with information technologies. This instruction will be carried out by two professional webmasters. The second purpose of these workshops will be to familiarize these staff members with the new print and online resources identified and compiled as part of this project and with effective pedagogical models and strategies for making use of these resources on their campuses. **Estimated annual cost: $80,000.**

Identification, Compilation, and Dissemination of Print/Electronic Resources: The staff and students will continue to expand their ongoing project to identify, compile, and disseminate print/electronic materials and related bibliographic information relating to the histories and cultures of subaltern racial, ethnic, and national groups as well as to the history and dynamics of ascribed status inequality in all its forms. The costs for this component will consist of the expenses involved in acquiring resources and student worker salaries for bibliographic research, compilation, and creation of print and electronic records. **Estimated annual cost: $40,000.**

Creation of Online Courses and Pedagogical Materials: Webmasters will create a series of online courses and pedagogical materials covering the histories and cultures of all groups on the campuses involved. **Estimated annual cost: $60,000.**

Total Project Cost: $180,000 per year, $540,000 for Three Years.

■ **Key Tasks for Rural Hospital Senior Transportation Project** (request to foundation):
1. Purchase van and hire driver for the Senior Transportation Project.
2. Schedule daily weekday hospital van pickup services for up to 50 elderly residents diagnosed with Alzheimer's disease who have no other mode of transportation to the hospital's Senior Day Care Program.

Budget Narrative

Major Property and Equipment Acquisition – $40,000
The hospital foundation will purchase one 15-passenger van. A regional auto dealer has agreed to sell us the van at cost. The sticker price is $60,000.

Van Driver – $24,000
The hospital foundation will hire one commercially licensed van driver to work a three-hour morning shift and a three-hour afternoon shift to pick up and drop off seniors attending the program. This will be a contracted position with no fringe benefits.

Van Expenses – $30,000
The hospital foundation is estimating that the annual fuel costs will be $15,000 and the maintenance costs not covered by the new vehicle warranty will be $5,000. Insurance on the van will cost $10,000.

■ **Key Tasks for High School Band Uniforms** (request to local businesses):
During the next school year, the band will perform at eight high school football games and six international festivals

where they will be required to wear concert uniforms pur-chased in 1972.

Budget Narrative

Kauai High School Band Boosters will use the requested monies to purchase 170 new concert uniforms at a dis-counted price of $30,000. The uniforms will be made of waterproof and stainproof material. The lifespan of the uniforms is 10 years. The manufacturer will also include 500 extra gold-plated buttons at no charge. These buttons normally sell for $3 each.

■ **Key Tasks for Camp Art and Music Therapy Program** (request to corporation):

1. Hire art and music therapist(s) to design learning and enrichment curriculum models for physically and men-tally challenged campers.

2. Purchase materials and supplies for six summer camp-ing sessions and for four winter wilderness fun camping sessions.

3. Videotape selected camping sessions for families, care-givers, and corporate supporters and for possible broadcast on several television stations around the state.

4. Photograph campers during the art and music therapy classes so that each camper can leave the camping ses-sion with a personal souvenir book containing pictures of all of his or her fun camp experiences.

Budget Narrative

Contracted Services – $32,000. Identify and contract with one art therapist and one music therapist who will agree to reside at Camp Civitan for 12 weeks each summer and four weeks each winter. (Room and board are free.) These therapists will be responsible for designing curriculum modules that can be used to teach highly challenged teens and older youths how to make art objects to support their ongoing developmental needs and how to use music as a way of improving their mobility, moods, and communications with others.

Materials and Supplies – $18,000. Purchase art and music therapy supplies to accommodate six two-week camping sessions and four one-week camping sessions for a total of 16 seven-day sessions. Each session has a pre-registration of 100 campers. Art materials and supplies include paper, canvas, poster board, assorted paints, inks, markers, pencils, charcoals, chalks, fabrics, string, adhesives, clay, wood, glazes, wire, bendable metals, and natural items (like shells, leaves, etc.). In addition, the following ability-appropriate tools will be purchased and used by students under close supervision: scissors, brushes, erasers, and easels. Supply trays, glue guns, smocks or aprons (reusable), and cleaning materials are also essential. Music materials and supplies include a boom box, CDs, and DVDs, which will be used for multiple camping seasons. In addition, purchase 1,600 photo albums so that each camper can take home memories to last until the next camping season.

Equipment – $1,000. Purchase karaoke equipment and television with DVD player and portable stand for classroom use. Also, purchase digital video camera with still-shot capability. All equipment will be used for multiple camping seasons.

Total Amount Requested: $51,000.

- **Key Tasks for Book Publishing Project** (request to corporation):

1. Complete 400-page book manuscript, *My Life Through Age 10,* by traveling to six countries and capturing the life stories of refugee children.

2. Submit completed manuscript to publishing houses to query their interest in signing a contract.

3. Set up nonprofit foundation so that proceeds from book sales are donated to orphanages in each of the countries and regions included in the book.

From beginning the travel to setting up the foundation, this is a 36-month project.

Budget Narrative

$395,000 (Years 1, 2, and 3): Contracted staff for the project—author, photographer, author's assistant, literary consultant, and nonprofit management consultant.

Author – $60,000 x 3 years = $180,000

Photographer – $20,000 x 1 year (Year 1) = $20,000

Assistant – $30,000 x 3 years = $90,000

Literary Consultant – $25,000 x 3 years = $75,000

Nonprofit Management Consultant – $30,000 x 1 year (Year 3) = $30,000

Subtotal for Contracted Staff: Year 1 – $135,000, Year 2 – $115,000, and Year 3 – $145,000

$30,000 (Years 1, 2, and 3): Office and production expenses calculated at $10,000 per year. Includes office supplies, photography supplies, courier services, telephone, Internet connectivity, rent, insurance, and Web site development.

Subtotal for Office and Production Expenses: Year 1 – $10,000, Year 2 – $10,000, and Year 3 – $10,000.

$40,000 (Year 1): Travel expenses include travel for the author, the photographer, and the assistant to visit Malawi, Namibia, Sudan, Uzbekistan, Bhutan, and Cambodia.

Subtotal for Travel Expenses: Year 1: $40,000.

Total Project Request: Year 1 – $185,000, Year 2 – $125,000, and Year 3 – $155,000, for a Total Request of $465,000.

■ **Key Tasks for Charter School 21st-Century Community Learning Centers** (request to government agency):

1. Formalize partnerships with community agencies (PAL), area churches via a mentoring program using Project Hope, and the school district.

2. Grow the Pathfinder Alternative Education program by providing additional renovation to the current site at district expense so that a school-age mother program can be housed there. This site, in addition to providing an online high school completion program, will offer parenting instruction contracted with the district using Safe Schools funds and parent training in literacy for parents using Title One funds.

3. Enable parents and children at Safe Schools sites to broaden their life experiences by participating in field trips to cultural and educational agencies statewide.

Budget Narrative

CATEGORY

Personnel

Project Coordinator (1.0 FTE, 12 months) @ $50,000

Community Liaison (1.0 FTE, 12 months) @ $40,000

Project Site Supervisors (5 positions, 1.0 FTE, 12 months) @ $25,000 = $125,000

Total Personnel Expenses: $215,000

Fringe Benefits

FICA, health insurance, retirement contribution matches, unemployment insurance, and workers' compensation @ 30% of personnel salaries = $64,500

Total Fringe Benefits Expenses: $64,500

Travel

Local travel for project staff is estimated at 200 miles monthly: total of $300 per month x 12 months = $3,600.

Field trips for Safe Schools parents and children via school buses. One field trip will be scheduled monthly for eight months. The cost per field trip is estimated at $1,000; this includes contracted transportation services, lunch, snacks on the bus, and admission fees. (The non-transportation items are included because grant application guidelines indicate that travel and travel-related expenses should be included under this category.) Field trips cost estimate: $8,000.

Total Travel Expenses: $11,600

Equipment

None.

Total Equipment Expenses: $0

Supplies

Site supplies for each of the curriculum models used with students and parents. The Business Manager has estimated that costs per site will be $3,500, x five sites = $17,500.

Total Supplies Expenses: $17,500

Contractual

The district will contract with a third-party evaluation firm, BBA, to carry all grant-funded objectives. The evaluator has submitted a pending bid offer that amounts to 15% of the total Direct Expenses for this grant application. This amount was derived by multiplying 15% x the subtotal for all other line items in Direct Costs: $408,600 x 15% = $61,290.

Total Contractual Expenses: $61,290

Construction

Under the allowable activities for this grant funding is the renovation of 21st Century Community Learning Center sites to accommodate parent education centers. The district will contract with a local construction firm to remove walls and/or build out each site's small community rooms by 1,000 additional square feet. The cost per site is $20,000, x 5 sites = $100,000.

Total Construction Expenses: $100,000

Total Direct Costs: $469,890.

Indirect Costs – The district's pre-negotiated indirect cost rate is 3.15%. $469,890 x 3.15% = $14,802.

Total Indirect Costs: $14,802.

Total Project Costs: $484,692.

- **Key Tasks for Statewide Injury Prevention Program** (request to government agency):

1. Building community support throughout the state for local injury prevention efforts through collaboration with community safety experts by conducting 30 information sessions and three leadership seminars each year.

2. Expanding implementation of injury prevention programs to include 25 elementary and middle schools each year.

3. Educating 500 teachers each year about the positive safety decisions students make and the ease of correlating the curriculum in the classroom.

4. Focusing educational efforts on the eight highest-risk areas for children—motor vehicle safety, fire and burn prevention, poisoning prevention, falls prevention, firearms prevention, bike and pedestrian safety, water safety, and choking, suffocation, and strangulation prevention.

5. Providing ongoing technical assistance, injury statistics, educational ideas, and legislative changes to schools currently using our intervention model.

Budget Narrative

CATEGORY

Personnel

Principal Investigator – 0.10 FTE x $100,000 per year = $10,000

Project Manager – 1.0 FTE x $50,000 per year = $50,000

Training Coordinator – 1.0 FTE x $40,000 per year = $40,000

Outreach Coordinator – 0.5 FTE x $45,000 per year = $22,250

Project Assistant – 0.33 FTE x $45,000 per year = $15,000

Total Personnel: $137,250

Fringe Benefits

Standard institutional benefits for staff working at least 30 hours per week: Project Manager, Training Coordinator, and Outreach Coordinator. Their salaries total $112,250, x 35% for fringe benefits = $39,288.

Total Fringe Benefits: $39,288

Travel

In-State: Project staff travel for training, education, home visits, and grant-related meetings. This figure was calculated using an annual mileage reimbursement of $3,900 each for four staff members, for a total annual cost of $15,600.

Out-of-State: The grantmaking agency requires that the Principal Investigator and Project Manager attend a three-day grantee orientation meeting in Washington, DC and also a five-day national evaluation meeting in Los Angeles, CA. Travel costs include airfare, hotel, meals, ground transportation, and miscellaneous costs that might arise during the team's travel. The total for both trips is $6,000.

Total Travel: $21,600

Educational Supplies

This $45,000 line item includes manuals for leadership seminars, materials for community leaders, resource boxes, questionnaires, 2,000 smoke detectors and long-lasting batteries, 4,000 drawer locks, 7,500 outlet covers, and 3,000 extension cords.

Total Educational Supplies: $45,000

Office Supplies

This $5,000 line item includes telephone service, postage, printing, faxing, and miscellaneous office-related needs.

Total Office Supplies: $5,000

Direct Costs: $248,138

Indirect Costs: The negotiated indirect cost rate is 15%. $248,138 x 15% = $37,221.

Total Budget: $285,359.

- **Key Tasks for Faith-Based Organization Capacity-Building Project** (request to government agency):
  1. Enable the volunteer Executive Director to be fully paid for program work.
  2. Hire a full-time Community Programs Coordinator.
  3. Upgrade the basketball equipment in the gymnasium for community use.

Budget Narrative

Personnel

Executive Director @ 1.0 FTE x $80,000 per year for 3 years: $240,000

Program Coordinator @ 1.0 FTE x $60,000 per year for 3 years: $180,000

Total Personnel: Year 1 – $140,000, Year 2 – $140,000, and Year 3 – $140,000. Total: $420,000.

Fringe Benefits

FICA, medical, retirement, and disability for full-time staff @ 25% of salaries.

Total Fringe Benefits: Year 1 – $35,000, Year 2 – $35,000, and Year 3 – $35,000. Total: $105,000.

Travel

County travel for program staff to market the Center's programs. Mileage will be reimbursed at 42.5 cents per mile for an estimated 250 miles per month x 12 months over the three-year project period. Calculated at $106.25 per month x 12 for an annual total of $1,275.

Total Travel: Year 1 – $1,275, Year 2 – $1,275, and Year 3 – $1,275. Total: $3,825.

Equipment

Basketball equipment: Ceiling-suspended rear-fold basketball backstops with glass backboard, bolt-on safety pads, breakaway rims and nets, electric winch, key switch, and auto-lock safety strap. Price includes installation and all electrical work. This equipment is needed to attract and accommodate weekend church basketball leagues, which will pay an annual facility use fee to help cover general operating expenses. Total cost for equipment upgrade: $12,000.

Total Equipment: Year 1 – $12,000

Total Direct Costs:

Year 1 – $188,275

Year 2 – $176,275

Year 3 – $176,275

Indirect Costs: None. At this time, the grant applicant has not agreed on an indirect cost rate with the Office of Management and Budget. This process is pending.

Total Budget: $540,725

2. Include Your Organization's and Its Partners' Cash and In-Kind Contributions

■ **For an International Wellness Research Institute** (request to foundation): A local management corporation, Accounting Now, has agreed to provide monthly financial tracking for all grant monies. In addition, Accounting Now will perform the annual audit. This in-kind contribution is valued at $12,000.

■ **For a Post-Secondary Capacity-Building Project** (request to foundation): Community partners will provide meeting space in four of the selected meeting regions. This value of space for 60 persons at each session, eight hours a day for three days in each of the four training segments, is $4,800. Air South has agreed to discount its fares for our members so that they can fly to the regional trainings. The total value of the air fare discounts for members traveling to the four regions is $36,000. We were unable to add an indirect cost rate to our budget (disallowed cost under grantmaker guidelines); therefore the University will cover the indirect cost expenses for the project. The value is $32,000.

■ **For a Rural Hospital Senior Transportation Project** (request to foundation): The Low Country Community Foundation has committed monies to pay for the van driver and for the van's fuel, insurance, and maintenance expenses over the next three years. This contribution amounts to $162,000.

■ **For High School Band Uniforms** (request to local businesses): A local dry cleaner has volunteered to clean the band's uniforms free of charge for the first five years. This is valued at $19,040 per year (for the eight games and festivals), for a total of $95,200 for the five-year period.

- **For a Camp Art and Music Therapy Program** (request to corporation): The Civitan Foundation is providing the facility for the annual sessions. The space used for the indoor and outdoor therapy courses is approximately 1,000 square feet. The commercial value of this size of classroom space, if leased, is $4,000 monthly, times four months equals $16,000. The prorated value of the electricity, water, and custodial expenses for this project is $15,000 for the camping season. The Foundation is not asking for these monies from the granting agency; it will cover these expenses from camper fees and other funding sources.

- **For a Book Publishing Project** (request to corporation): In the past, the author has earned as much as $200,000 annually in royalties and through her work with a hit pay-for-view show. However, during the course of this project, the author will not be able to work on any other publications or honor her film contract. This means that the author is actually donating most of her time on this project. She is contributing approximately $120,000 per year over the course of three years to guarantee completing and publishing the book and achieving record-breaking sales.

- **For Charter School 21st Century Community Learning Centers** (request to government agency): Under the charter school's contract with the authorizing school district, the district has agreed to match up to 20% of any capital improvements made to our campuses. The federal request for $100,000 to build our five parent education centers will be matched by the district at $20,000. This will enable our charter school to install state-of-the-art training equipment and a security system to protect the computer lab and other equipment and furnishings from theft or vandalism.

- **For a Statewide Injury Prevention Program** (request to government agency): The University houses the Center and does not charge for use of the 5,000 square feet of office and meeting space. The value of this in-kind contribution is $10,000 per month times 12 months for a total of $120,000 annually. Prorated utilities, maintenance, and administrative parking spaces (every employee pays to park in the staff garage) is $40,000 annually.

- **For a Faith-Based Organization Capacity-Building Project** (request to government agency): We're asking for a capacity-building grant because our internal resources are minimal. However, we have 20 faithful volunteers who work an average of 10 hours weekly year-round. This commitment totals to 10,400 hours. According to Independent Sector (www.independentsector.org), the hourly value of a volunteer, nationally, is $18.04. This means that our volunteers are valued at $187,616 annually!

3. Provide Funders with a Solid Plan for Sustainability

- **For an International Wellness Research Institute** (request to foundation): While we will charge participating Centers around the world for the workshops, there will not be a profit on this effort. However, we have retained the services of SCORE to help us design a higher revenue-producing training program so that future expenses will be covered by participants.

- **For a Post-Secondary Capacity-Building Project** (request to foundation): Once this project is funded, the ongoing expense will be for the webmaster who will keep the online content updated and the asynchronous environment running. Once we have perfected the project, community partners have committed to supporting the webmaster's salary and fringe benefits.

- **For a Rural Hospital Senior Transportation Project** (request to foundation): The project will be sustained by the hospital's foundation, which will raise the needed funds annually from the auxiliaries to pay for the driver's salary and vehicle-related expenses.

- **For High School Band Uniforms** (request to local businesses): Under the direction of the new band director, the band will begin to plan and implement annual fundraisers (pancake breakfasts, raffles, and play-a-thons). The funds raised will be deposited into a money management account with higher interest rates. By the time new uniforms are needed, the funds will be in place.

- **For a Camp Art and Music Therapy Program** (request to corporation): The Civitan Foundation of the Southwest will aggressively continue to seek private sector donors to support the annual expenses for the Art and Music Therapy Program.

- **For a Book Publishing Project** (request to corporation): Once the grant funding period has ended, there will be no need for future funding. The revenues from the book will be used for charitable purposes, as stated earlier in this budget narrative.

- **For Charter School 21st Century Community Learning Centers** (request to government agency): The district will continue to pursue other means of funding to sustain the programs. We will also look at current funding to redesign programs that were piloted in the 21st century. We will look to business and industry for assistance as well as tuition fees. Once the programs prove their worth to the community, the community will be motivated to find ways to support and sustain them. We, as a district, are always pursuing creative funding and we commit an administrator's salary plus office support to continue that pursuit.

- **For a Statewide Injury Prevention Program** (request to government agency): The Center will continue to aggressively pursue public and private sector funding opportunities to continue to expand the sites using our prevention methodologies. Once the success and magnitude of our program reach the national media, we expect interested funders to contact us about supporting our efforts.

■ **For a Faith-Based Organization Capacity-Building Project** (request to government agency): The anticipated program income will bring in $22,000 annually. While this will not fully cover the annual operating costs, it will allow us to retain the services of a grant writer who will aggressively search and apply for other grant funding opportunities.

How Will You Know How Much to Write for the Budget Section?

Follow the grantmaker's guidelines for page limitation specifications. In the budget narrative, providing lots of detail is the best approach so that you can justify spending someone else's monies.

Chapter 12
Applicant Agency Structure:
Talking About Your
Board of Directors

Did you know that many private sector funders (foundations and corporations) look very closely at your Board of Directors' profiles? They scrutinize the Board roster and look for specific "revealing" information that helps them decide if the members have the following characteristics: 1) they have diverse occupations, 2) they do not all have the same last name and address, 3) they represent various populations in your service area, 4) their terms are short enough to ensure frequent changes in thinking and ideas, and 5) they rotate the responsibilities of the Executive Committee (President, Vice President, Secretary, and Treasurer).

A good grant writer can spin a tale of woe to create the Needs Statement. We can tell a story to write an award-winning program design. We can also scrutinize the budget and make sure that there are no red flags. However, we cannot save what would have been a winning proposal if the Board of Directors roster is missing the perfect phrases needed to pass funder scrutiny. You'll finish this chapter with new insight into how to help your organization or client develop a Board of Directors roster that passes funder inspection—every time!

Elements of a Winning Board of Directors Roster

1. List Your Board of Directors by Name, Board Title, and Occupation.
2. Show Board Member Demographics and Terms of Service.
3. Provide Funders with Board Duties.

1. List Your Board of Directors by Name, Board Title, and Occupation

■ **For Homeless Shelter:**

1. Jennifer Mitchell, President. Director, State of Arizona Office of Children and Family Services.
2. Mason Ahn Crawford, Vice President. Owner and manager, 15 state-funded non-secure residential facilities for youth, ages 6 to 17 years old.
3. Lorraine Bryant, Secretary. Director, Gila County Foster Parents Association.
4. Jalen Strong, Treasurer. Former homeless teen, now Executive Director, Children's Trust Fund of Arizona.
5. Mack Jackson, Member. Retired Gila County Juvenile Probation Officer.
6. Jessica Lee, Member. Juvenile Court Judge, Gila County.

■ **For Hospital Foundation:**

1. Dr. Allen Nelson, President. Chief of Staff, McDonald West Medical Center.
2. Dr. Patricia Baker, Vice President. Head of Pediatric Neurosurgery, Jefferson County Hospital.
3. Dr. Ari Pax, Secretary. Geriatric Specialist, private practice.
4. Ella Neal, Treasurer. Former Head of Nursing, Wyoming Facility for the Mentally Insane.
5. Keith Wright, Member. Executive Director, Wyoming Area Hospice Centers.
6. Max Weinstein, Member. Deputy Director, Wyoming Children's Hospital.

7. Jillian Mobley, Member. Operations Manager, North Country Cancer Association.
8. Maxie Cartwright, Member. President, McDonald West Medical Center Auxiliary.
9. Kerry Kirkpatrick, Member. Certified Public Accountant.
10. Robert Chuchip, Member. Director, Tribal Council.

■ **For Chamber of Commerce:**

1. Larry Ford, President. Entrepreneurial Startup Consultant.
2. Charles S. Mott, III, Vice President. Director, CS3 Foundation.
3. Mary Elizabeth Wells, Secretary. Research Librarian, Michigan Business Owners Association.
4. Abu Muhammad, Treasurer. Assistant Branch Manager, Genesee Bank.
5. Ricardo Martinez, Member. Owner, Martinez Design Services.
6. Hillary James, Member. Programming Director, WJRF.
7. Michael Bertinelli, Member. Owner, Bertinelli Glass Works.
8. Dr. Haley Mickelson, Member. Chancellor, University of Michigan—Flint Campus.
9. Jeffery Burns, Member. Director, City of Flint Office of Economic Development.

■ **For Bristol-Warren Regional School District:**

1. Dr. Nehemiah Rice, President. Assistant Chancellor, Warren Community College.
2. Edith Eaton, Vice President. Director, Bristol-Warren Skill Center.

3. Henry Wise, Secretary. Director, Downtown Development Association.

4. Mercedes Updike, Treasurer. President, Bristol-Warren Historical Society.

5. Ellsworth Biddle, Member. Owner, custodial business; parent of six children enrolled in District schools.

6. Sierra Lynn Danbury, Member. Retired owner, bed and breakfast; grandparent of four children enrolled in District schools.

7. Ricardo Esteban, Member. Retired District teacher; foster parent to 12 children enrolled in District schools.

8. Glory Beth Berry, Member. Owner, floral shop.

9. Terry Thomas, Youth-at-Large Member. Honor Society student, Warren High School.

■ **For Cave Creek Zoological Society:**

1. Phoebe Masterson, President. Doctor of Veterinary Medicine and owner, local veterinary clinic.

2. Jim Jackson, Vice President. Former Governor, State of New Mexico.

3. Farnsworth Brooks, Secretary. Executive Director, Las Cruces Animal Shelter.

4. Suzanne Pettit, Treasurer. Volunteer, Cave Creek Friends of the Zoo Association.

5. Carolyn Munoz, Member. Director, Hispania Familias for Life.

6. Carlos Izquierdo, Member. Executive Director, Los Cruces Community Foundation.

7. Hesper Valdez, Member. Assistant Director, New Mexico Farm Bureau.

Applicant Agency Structure

- **For AmiCan Night Vision:**
  1. JoAnne Wood, President. Director, Search & Rescue Research Laboratories.
  2. Marcus Steiner, Vice President. Patent Attorney, private practice.
  3. Ruben Redford, Secretary. Former Director, Federal Emergency Management Administration.
  4. Helga Olgeson, Treasurer. Former member, Soviet Union Security Command.
  5. Jefferson Star, Member-at-Large. Gulf War Veteran. Former Navy Seals team member.

- **For the Uptown Urban League:**
  1. Livingston Williams, President. Executive Director, Chicago Minority Business Development Council.
  2. Cheryl Jean Sessoms, Vice President. Special Advisor, Mayor's Office on Equality, City of Chicago.
  3. Ralph Martin, Secretary. Owner, Martin Security Systems.
  4. Victoria Valdez, Treasurer. Chancellor, Uptown University.
  5. Richard Hill, Member. Director of Trust Funds, Uptown Bank.
  6. Sheldon Sparks, Member. Founder, Midlines Air.
  7. Allison Conyers, Member. Former Congressional member, 108th Congress.

- **For the Town of Goose Creek:**
  Note: The Town is a unit of municipal government. It does not have a Board of Directors; it is governed by an elected Town Council.
  1. Jessie Mae Stevens, Mayor of Goose Creek.

2. Marley Jefferson, Vice Mayor of Goose Creek.
3. Hills Jenkins, Council Representative for District 1. Retired automotive manufacturing worker.
4. Cecelia Edwards, Council Representative for District 2. Accountant, Delray and Associates.
5. Sara Shopkow, Council Representative for District 3. Superintendent, Goose Creek Public Schools.
6. Hattie Harrison, Council Representative for District 4. Homemaker and community activist.
7. Addison Stillwell, Council Representative for District 5. Retired fire chief, Town of Goose Creek.
8. Karen Wright, Council Representative for District 6. Owner, six McHamburger franchises in Goose County.

- **For St. Raphael Church Building Fund:**

1. Jill Henderson, President. Director, Stevensville Roman Catholic Diocese.
2. Ramon Garcia, Vice President. Custodian, St. Raphael Church.
3. Dr. John Becker, Secretary. Retired family practice physician.
4. Jake Vito, Treasurer. Owner, Little Sicily's Pizza Parlor.
5. Mary Korana, Member. Owner, Mary's Day Care Center.
6. Bargamy Jones, Member. Pastor, Hillside Roman Catholic Church.
7. Rose Mary Armstrong, Member. Health care worker, Catholic Medical Systems.
8. Charles Scott, Member. Manager, Deluxe Financial Collections, Inc.
9. Donald Jacobson, Member. Chairperson, St. Raphael's Women's Auxiliary.

10. Catherine Bevis, Member. Owner, Cathy's Pastry Shoppe.
11. Deborah Porsche, Member. Assistant Manager, Wal-Mart Distribution Center.
12. Minnie Lee Elliott, Member. Switchboard Operator, Dollar General Corporation.

■ **For Nebraska League of Cities and Towns:**

1. Romero Vargas, President. Mayor, City of Circle Grove.
2. Halle Blue, Vice President. Mayor, City of Lincoln.
3. Andrew Anderson, Secretary. Mayor, Creek Village.
4. Beatrice Nixon, Treasurer. Mayor, City of Jenkins.
5. Zed Smothers, Member. Mayor, City of Ainsworth.
6. Rabias Krebs, Member. Mayor, City of Scottsbluff.
7. Ravenna Callaway, Member. Mayor, City of Grand Island.
8. Hiram Chogan, Member. Tribal Director, Winnebago Indian Reservation.
9. Winifred Verdigre, Member. Tribal Housing Director, Santee Indian Reservation.

2. Show Board Member Demographics and Terms of Service

■ **For Homeless Shelter:**

The Shelter has six Board members. The ethnicities represented include Caucasian, Korean, African American, and Thai. Three members are women and three are men. The members range in age from 25 to 72 years old. All Board terms are for two years. The President and Secretary are elected on the even years and the Vice President and Treasurer are elected on the odd years. Officers may not be elected for more than two consecutive terms. Members-at-large may be elected for up to three consecutive terms.

■ **For Hospital Foundation:**

The Foundation has 10 Board members. Five are female and five are male. Only two of the Board members are affiliated with the McDonald West Medical Center. Three members are physicians and one is a mental health nurse. Two Board members represent statewide health affiliates. Of the 10 members, four represent minority stakeholders. Each member serves a two-year term. The terms are staggered annually to preserve continuity or management. Elected directors serve as individuals, regardless of their affiliation or employment.

■ **For Chamber of Commerce:**

The Chamber Board is composed of nine dedicated volunteers. Members represent business, education, finance, and nonprofit management. The Board has five males and four females. Currently, we have a vacant position that is desig-nated for a female member; we expect to begin accepting nominations for this vacancy at the next Board meeting (next month on the 15th). Our Board is diverse and repre-sents an ethnic cross section of the community. Members represent the Jewish, African American, Hispanic, Italian, and Arabic communities. Elections are held every year, to encourage new members of the community to serve on one of the highest-profile Boards in our state. Current members may not serve for two consecutive terms.

- **For Bristol-Warren Regional School District:**
The District has nine publicly elected Board members. The election is held every two years and is open to all eligible voters and residents of both Bristol and Warren Townships. The one Board member who is not elected in this manner is the Youth-at-Large member. This member is always a high school junior who is elected in school-wide elections held at Warren and Bristol High Schools. Interested students develop campaign messages and address full assemblies at both high schools. It is a very positive learning experience for our students and it also demonstrates the civic process. Three past Youth-at-Large members have gone on to the state university and majored in Political Science. One former Youth-at-Large member is now the Mayor of Bristol. The remaining Board members represent all segments of the community. There is equal gender representation (not counting the Youth-at-Large member, who is male). Several minority groups are also represented as well as two members who represent

Rhode Island's founding families who settled Bristol and Warren.

■ **For Cave Creek Zoological Society:**

Seven members make up our Board of Directors. Four are female and three are male. Our area has a high population of Latinos, so three of our Board members are of Hispanic origin. Collectively, the Board represents broad segments of the community, from animal-related organizations to Latino families to the Community Foundation. Board members serve three-year terms. Elections are held every two years, providing overlapping of terms to ensure continuity and experience on the Board. New members are encouraged to nominate others who might be interested in our cause. Our bylaws allow for up to 15 Board members. We hope to reach our maximum in the next six years.

■ **For AmiCan Night Vision:**

AmiCan is a privately owned international research corporation that is honored to have five stellar, world-renowned Board members. Two are female and three are male. The members have varying levels of expertise in law, search-and-rescue research, national-level emergency management protocol, foreign military affairs, and homeland defense. The members serve four-year terms and must rotate officer positions annually so that no one member assumes a dominant leadership role for more than 12 months. The Board represents our customers and venture capitalists (who helped to start our company five years ago) who have a high interest in advanced defense technologies.

- **For the Uptown Urban League:**

  The League's Board is representative of its city-wide constituency. Our seven dedicated professionals represent minority businesses, public equality policymakers, private micro enterprises, minority-held banks, higher education, and government. The membership is 80% minority—six of the seven members are minorities. Three members are female and four are male. Members are elected for six-year terms and elections are staggered so that there are always members with experience.

- **For the Town of Goose Creek:**

  The Town Council is elected every two years by the public. Candidates run in each of the six districts; those receiving the most votes are elected to the Council. In addition, the Mayor and Vice Mayor also serve on the Council. Their terms are for four years and they are also elected by the public. Each district is a unique cosmopolitan mixture of special interest groups and minority subpopulations. District 1 is predominantly African American. District 2 is a small neighborhood of Rastafarians. Districts 4 and 5 have multiple subpopulations, with Caucasian being the largest group represented. District 6 is known as our Haitian Village.

- **For St. Raphael Church Building Fund:**

  The 12 members of our Board are dedicated to helping us reach our Building Fund goals. Females and males are equally represented. Our Board is probably one of the most diverse in the Diocese in terms of racial mix (60% are minorities) and community cross sections. 75% of the members are working in a management capacity and lend their varying levels of expertise to our campaign. Board terms are for two years, with staggered elections for those on the Executive Committee. Four of the 12 members are over the age of 55 years old. Our members reflect the communities we serve and our parishioners as well.

- **For Nebraska League of Cities and Towns:**
The League's bylaws (adopted from the National League of Cities) require that all Boards of Directors be composed of elected officials from local units of municipal government including Tribal nations. There are two large reservations in Nebraska, the Winnebago and the Santee Indian Reservations. One elected Tribal member from each reservation serves on the League's current Board. In addition, seven positions are held by Mayors of Nebraska cities, ranging from small communities with fewer than 3,000 residents to large urban areas, like Lincoln, whose population is 239,213. Board members are elected to two-year terms. Members and officers of the Executive Committee are determined by all League members at the League's Annual Conference through a process coordinated by a Nominating Committee.

3. Provide Funders with Board Duties

■ **For Board President or Chairperson or Director:**

1. Has served as a member prior to being elected as an officer.
2. Is willing to provide leadership to the Board of Directors.
3. Understands Robert's Rules of Order.
4. Understands the level of accountability between the Executive Director and the Board Officers.
5. Is willing to lead Executive Committee (top elected officers) in making Executive Director hiring and firing decisions.
6. Develops the agenda and chairs meetings.
7. Delegates responsibilities to the Vice President or Vice Chair if absent.
8. Makes a personal or corporate financial contribution to the organization or entity the Board oversees.
9. Is willing to solicit financial support of others in the community to help the organization or entity it oversees progress toward sustainability.
10. Maintains confidentiality at all times.
11. Represents the Board and organization publicly without negativity.
12. Participates in annual organizational strategic planning process.
13. Performs other responsibilities as defined in the bylaws.

■ **For the Vice President or Vice Chair:**

1. Has served as a member prior to being elected as an officer.

2. Is willing to provide leadership to the Board of Directors.

3. Regularly attends Board meetings.

4. Understands Robert's Rules of Order.

5. Understands the level of accountability between the Executive Director and the Board Officers.

6. Is willing to lead Executive Committee (top elected officers) in making Executive Director hiring and firing decisions.

7. Makes a personal or corporate financial contribution to the organization or entity the Board oversees.

8. Is willing to solicit financial support of others in the community to help the organization or entity it oversees progress toward sustainability.

9. Maintains confidentiality at all times.

10. Represents the Board and organization publicly without negativity.

11. Participates in annual organizational strategic planning process.

12. Performs other responsibilities as defined in the bylaws.

■ **For the Secretary:**

1. Has served as a member prior to being elected as an officer.

2. Regularly attends Board meetings.

3. Records the Board meeting minutes, makes corrections, and enters them into the official records for the Board.

4. Works with organization's staff to print copies of past and current meeting minutes and have them sent to Board members 14 days prior to the meeting date.

5. Prepares and maintains roster of all Board members with most current contact information.

6. Collects biographies on all Board members for inclusion into official records and Board member profile files (maintained by the organization).
7. Signs all official Board correspondence.
8. Is able to notarize organization's public documents.
9. Is responsible for filing annual corporate reports with state agencies.
10. Is responsible for updating bylaws.
11. Is responsible for amending Articles of Corporation if changes are approved by the Executive Committee.
12. Makes a personal or corporate financial contribution to the organization or entity the Board oversees.
13. Is willing to solicit financial support of others in the community to help the organization or entity it oversees progress toward sustainability.
14. Maintains confidentiality at all times.
15. Represents the Board and organization publicly without negativity.
16. Participates in annual organizational strategic planning process.
17. Performs other responsibilities as defined in the bylaws.

- **For the Treasurer:**
  1. Has served as a member prior to being elected as an officer.
  2. Regularly attends Board meetings.
  3. Ensures that funds are property deposited and disbursed.
  4. Is able to prepare organization's financial statements and submit them for full Board approval.

5. Chairs Finance Committee.
6. Works with Board and staff to prepare and finalize annual operating budget.
7. Signs off on all documents relating to organization's finances, including grant applications and grant award agreements.
8. Understands the federal operating circulars as they relate to accounting practices for the specific types of organizations.
9. Contracts with independent certified public accountant to conduct annual audit.
10. Makes a personal or corporate financial contribution to the organization or entity the Board oversees.
11. Is willing to solicit financial support of others in the community to help the organization or entity it oversees progress toward sustainability.
12. Chairs Fundraising Committee.
13. Maintains confidentiality at all times.
14. Represents the Board and organization publicly without negativity.
15. Participates in annual organizational strategic planning process.
16. Performs other responsibilities as defined in the bylaws.

■ **For Board Members Who Are Not Officers:**
1. Regularly attends Board and Committee meetings.
2. Willing to accept assignments from Board officers.
3. Comes to Board meetings prepared, having read agenda, and introduces relevant topics to aid officers in Board business.

4. Makes a personal or corporate financial contribution to the organization or entity the Board oversees.
5. Is willing to solicit financial support of others in the community to help the organization or entity it oversees progress toward sustainability.
6. Maintains confidentiality at all times.
7. Represents the Board and organization publicly without negativity.
8. Participates in annual organizational strategic planning process.
9. Performs other responsibilities as defined in the bylaws.

How Do You Know How Much to Include About Your Board of Directors?

Always follow the funder's guidelines. If there are none, then this is the one section where you can include scads of relevant detail on your Board of Directors. Remember: information on your Board of Directors is usually requested under the Mandatory Attachments list. Do not incorporate this information into the grant proposal narrative unless the guidelines instruct you to write about the Board's qualifications in the Management Plan or the Program Design.

Chapter 13
Letters of Support:
Getting and Giving Winning Letters

This is the last chapter of *Perfect Phrases for Writing Grant Proposals*. I've had so much fun writing these phrases for you!

In this chapter, I will share some examples of perfect phrases for creating letters of support. These can be letters that your organization writes for its community partners or letters that you ask your partners to write for your own grant proposals. Either way, a generic template is out. Carefully phrased and placed facts to support specific applications and proposed programs are in. Let's get started!

Elements of Credible Letters of Support:

1. Develop a Purposeful Opening Paragraph.
2. Develop a Historical Relationship Paragraph.
3. Develop a Compelling Closing Paragraph.

1. Develop a Purposeful Opening Paragraph

In this paragraph, I want you to include three key components: the purpose of the letter, the name of your organization, and the name of the funding competition. For these examples, I want to focus on the areas where the most common types of grants are awarded. While I'm using the top government funding areas, these perfect phrases will help you write the same types of letters for corporate and foundation grantmakers.

- **For International Development Grants:**
  I am writing this letter to demonstrate support for Serenity Village's grant application to the USAID for the Emerging Sustainability Pilot Initiative.

- **For Community Services Grants:**
  On behalf of our Board of Directors, I am writing this letter to demonstrate our matching funds support for Nana's Lemonade Stand, Inc.'s grant application to the Corporation for National and Community Service—Youth Development Programs.

- **For Agriculture Grants:**
  This letter is to support the Concord Little League's grant application to the Michigan Department of Agriculture's discretionary grants program for Rural Sport Complexes.

- **For Commerce Grants:**
  Our organization is pleased to support the grant application being submitted by the Nebraska League of Cities and Towns to the U.S. Department of Commerce for the Public Administrator's Professional Development Program.

For Defense Grants:

The Board of Directors for Invisible Defenses, Inc. has passed a resolution to provide a letter of longstanding commitment for the United Kingdom Robotics grant application to the U.S. Department of Defense for its Unarmed Invasion Research Grant Program.

For Education Grants:

The Parent-Teacher Organization for Charleston Public Schools is excited to support the Charleston NRA Youth Club's application to the U.S. Department of Education 21st Century Community Learning Centers Grant Program.

For Energy Grants:

The State of Nevada's Governor's Office is writing this letter on behalf of the Nevada Energy Commission to support its grant application to the Turner Mega Energy Foundation for the Developing Solar Substations Grant Initiative.

For Health Grants:

The Blue Sky Medical Center is encouraged and excited to demonstrate support for the Smokey River Public Health Clinic's grant application to the Robert Wood Johnson Foundation's Public Health Centers Grant Program.

For Homeland Security Grants:

The City of Prescott Valley, Arizona, is writing this letter of support for Night Vision Systems, Inc. to support its grant application to the U.S. Department of Homeland Security for the U.S.-based Border Surveillance Technologies Grant Program.

- **For Housing Grants:**

  The Portland Housing Authority will support the Salmon River Transitional Shelter's grant application to the Oregon State Housing Authority for the Discretionary Housing Grant Program.

- **For Historic Preservation Grants:**

  The City of Jonesboro is writing this letter of support to demonstrate the critical need for Mid-South Health System's (MSHS) grant application to purchase the Old Marie McDonald House (circa 1800). The Saving America's Treasures Grant Program's priorities clearly match the use that MSHS intends for this property.

- **For Employment and Training Grants:**

  The Michigan National Bank Foundation is committing its financial resources to support the grant application submitted by Jobs Central to the Charles Stewart Mott Foundation for expanded programming at the Silverstone Skill Center.

- **For Transportation Grants:**

  The Toronto Chamber of Commerce Board of Directors has voted to support the Kid's Campus grant application to the Ministry of Transportation for the Youth Metro Transportation Grant Programme.

- **For Veterans Grants:**

  On behalf of the Hurley Medical Center's Board of Directors, the Chief of Staff has been authorized to write this letter of support for the Indianapolis Veterans Hospital's grant application to the U.S. Department of Veterans Affairs' Strengthening Outpatient Services Grant Program.

■ **For Environmental Grants:**

The Barton Creek Environmental Association is pleased to write a letter of support for the Texas Department of Environmental Services grant application to the National Fish and Wildlife Foundation for the Native Species Preservation Grant.

■ **For Museum and Library Grants:**

The State of Louisiana Department of Library Services is writing this letter to support the grant application to the Mercer Foundation being submitted by the Ninth Ward Historical Preservation Committee.

■ **For Aeronautics and Space Grants:**

Career Explosion is pleased to write this letter of support for the Kids Can Fly organization to aid in its pursuit of a grant award from the Constellation Foundation's Fly Now Grant Program.

■ **For Arts Grants:**

The City of Bedrock Council Authority has approved this letter of commitment for the Creative Expressions Dance Studio's grant application to the Johnson City Council for the Arts.

■ **For Humanities Grants:**

As Editor-in-Chief of *The Daily Journal*, I am pleased to write this letter of support for the Mt. Morris School District's Reader in the Classroom Program grant application to the North Dakota Council for the Humanities.

- **For Science Grants:**

  On behalf of the Chancellor's Office on Experiential Learning for the University of Baytown, I am writing this letter to support the Hands-On Science Center's application to the National Science Foundation.

2. Develop a Historical Relationship Paragraph

Provide grant readers with a sense of your partnership with the organization seeking grant funding.

■ **For International Development Grants:**
The International Institute has been a longstanding partner with Serenity Village. The Director and I have sat on multiple community boards and committees over the past 20 years. One of our former Board members, who is also an evaluation consultant, has completed several evaluations for Serenity Village's international aid programs. In two months, both of our organizations will be sharing a weekend capacity-building retreat and Board training event. This shared event will enable the Institute to write another five-year Memorandum of Agreement with Serenity Village for joint programming and training (cost-effective resource delivery) in developing countries.

■ **For Community Services Grants:**
We can remember when Nana's Lemonade Stand was formed seven years ago. Our faithful and everlasting alliance with Nana until her death has resulted in a 20-year lease with Nana's Board of Directors for free space in our complex for its administrative staff and classrooms or its international franchise training program.

■ **For Agriculture Grants:**
Mitchell Township has had a working relationship with the Concord Little League for 15 years. The township maintains the public ball fields that the League teams use each

spring and summer. The games bring many out-of-town visitors to our township and we benefit economically because of the positive presence of Concord Little League.

■ **For Commerce Grants:**

The National League of Cities and Towns was founded in 1927. Shortly after, the Nebraska League of Cities and Towns was founded. It was our first affiliate. Our relationship has prospered for decades. We have watched the Nebraska League grow and become a model for the country.

■ **For Defense Grants:**

United Kingdom Robotics (UKR) has been a subcontractor with Invisible Defenses, Inc. for 10 years. During this time, UKR has helped our corporation develop over $10 million in product lines for foreign nations. This partnership is further solidified by the recent development of a joint working agreement between UKR and our corporation.

■ **For Education Grants:**

In a region where the public schools close down for hunting season so teachers and students can head for the woods, it's not unusual for parents to want their children to learn gun handling safety. The PTO for Charleston Public Schools believes that our five-year partnership with the Charleston NRA Youth Club has been educational and life-saving for students who are given guns as gifts, but not given instructions on gun safety.

■ **For Energy Grants:**

The Governor's Office has historically been a key partner with the Nevada Energy Commission in its efforts to move our state into the next millennium without dependency on coal fuels or traditional electrical sources. Both the Governor and the Director for the Commission serve on the Joint Committee for Energy Conservation and have served the state together for 12 years.

■ **For Health Grants:**

We have been a key partner with the Smokey River Public Health Clinic since it was built in 1958. Most recently, the Clinic participated in the state's emergency drills, which took place on our grounds. Over 2,000 volunteers and medical professionals came together for this successful event. The drill demonstrated the impact that community partners can make when they join forces.

■ **For Homeland Security Grants:**

Night Vision Systems, Inc. has had a presence in our community since 2000. Their continuing efforts to be environmentally friendly, their active involvement in governmental affairs, and their ongoing support for the Humboldt Unified School District science classes has earned them the Good Neighbor Award from the Mayor of Prescott Valley.

■ **For Housing Grants:**

The Salmon River Transitional Shelter has answered our pleas for families in need of shelter and support services for the past 10 years—since they opened their Calumet Road facility.

■ **For Historic Preservation Grants:**

Mid-South Health Systems, Inc. has been a part of our community for 27 years. During this time, the City of Jonesboro has partnered with Mid-South multiple times to create pro-

Letters of Support

gramming for those in need of mental health services. Both agencies have met over the past five years to discuss how we can find additional space for mentally ill persons who need longer-term community-based care options. The McDonald House proposal is worthy of funding.

■ **For Employment and Training Grants:**
The Michigan National Bank Foundation has worked with employment and training agencies like Jobs Central since the days of the Comprehensive Employment and Training Act (before 1983). The Bank requests that the Foundation's Director sit on the Board of Directors for Jobs Central. This alliance has resulted in a greater economic impact on Tarrant County residents.

■ **For Transportation Grants:**
In our province and country, the theme has always been partnerships: make them and value them. The Chamber's longstanding partnership with Kid's Campus started in 1957 and is ongoing today.

■ **For Veterans Grants:**
For 20 years, Hurley Medical Center has had a reciprocal agreement for transferring veterans from our Burn Center and Psychiatric Unit to the Indianapolis Veterans Hospital. Our institutions share the same 10-block campus and depend on one another for sharing critically scarce resources.

■ **For Environmental Grants:**
The Association has worked hand in hand with the Texas Department of Environmental Services since our incorporation in 1958. This partnership has enabled our group to

receive over $5 million in competitive grant awards to restore Barton Creek.

- **For Museum and Library Grants:**
  The Mercer Foundation has been an aggressive partner in preserving Louisiana's heritage. We are proud to be their partner since 1992 and to support this new endeavor by the Foundation to preserve what is left of New Orleans' Ninth Ward.

- **For Aeronautics and Space Grants:**
  Kids Can Fly has partnered with Career Explosion for nearly two decades in the areas of grant funding and strategic planning. The most recent partnership activity was when our Boards of Directors and staffs together attended a national conference at Cape Kennedy. Our partnership continues to be strengthened by sharing resources.

- **For Arts Grants:**
  The Creative Expressions Dance Studio has occupied one of the city's athletic field houses for nearly 17 years free of charge. This relationship continues to prosper for the city, the Studio, and the inner-city youth who have been trained in dancing and etiquette by the Studio's dedicated staff.

- **For Humanities Grants:**
  Through the Newspapers in the Classroom Initiative, *The Daily Journal* has been a partner with the Mt. Morris School District for nearly 30 years.

- **For Science Grants:**
  The University's science faculty has been partnering with the Hands-on Science Center for nearly three years to help it develop its new virtual tunnel exhibit.

3. Develop a Compelling Closing Paragraph

- **Closing with Hope** (for funding):

1. Serenity Village's proposed international initiative has high merit and promising outcomes. A USAID grant award is the financial stimulus needed to reach out to developing countries needing new resources and education in using them. Serenity Village is one organization that can make significant positive strides in many small struggling developing areas outside of the United States.

2. Every weekend, I take my family to watch the Concord Little League play their games—at least during good weather, when nature does not cause the games to be canceled. With your support, the League will be able to move its events out of the elements and into a new sports facility. We are hopeful—for the children—that this facility will become a reality.

3. The League's professional development program for Nebraska's Chamber of Commerce members will enable an agency whose staff is trained to share their knowledge and approaches for successful Chamber management to build membership capacities statewide. We are awaiting positive news on this critically needed and worthy project.

4. United Kingdom Robotics (UKR) is the nation's leader in the wide field of unarmed invasion research. It is both reassuring and validating that a grant award will enable significant strides in this highly competitive area of defense research and development.

5. The 400 boys and girls on the waiting list to attend the NRA Youth Club eagerly await your positive decision that they will soon have a three-year fully funded 21st Century Community Learning Center in Charleston.

■ **Closing with Woe** (what happens if it's not funded!):

1. The grant award that Mid-South Health Systems is positioned to receive will mean the difference between leaving the mentally ill to roam the streets of Jonesboro and welcoming them in a tightly supervised community-based residential treatment center. Without grant funding, the City will have no choice but to pass an ordinance preventing the mentally ill from loitering on the streets. While this may seem inhumane, we have no alternative since funding is not plentiful and other local resources are scarce as well.

2. When we first envisioned Kid's Campus being able to provide transportation for inner-city youth traveling from their homes and schools to public recreation facilities after school and summers, we never thought that the City would not have the funds to support this vision. However, because our economy has been declining and our mass transportation system is overcrowded and often unsafe, youth face risks on the subways or busses. Without your funding support, the proposed Youth Metro Transportation Program will never materialize in the Province.

3. Barton Creek has come a long way from the decades of corporate waste pollution and dead fish floating for miles downstream. Yet, there is still need to restore

native species of fish to Barton Creek. Locally, and even in the state, there are no funds for such "frivolous" projects. The only funding source for this is you—the National Fish and Wildlife Foundation. Without your support, Barton Creek will eventually go back to being a stagnant body of water with no recreational value or purpose.

4. With state funding cuts annually for our public schools, it's a miracle that a small rural school district like Mt. Morris can still be recognized for its exemplary academics and dedicated educators. The Reader in the Classroom Program is critically needed to enable visiting English Language Arts scholars to read to young children with limited English speaking skills. Without this grant, the district will be forced to deny grade promotion for students who cannot meet the ELA requirements for grade progression.

5. Nevada is growing faster than any other state. The demand for electricity is at an all-time high for the cities that never sleep (Las Vegas, Laughlin, Reno, and Searchlight). Statewide, the energy consumption by these 24-hour gaming destinations has taken its toll on our energy reserves. Without this grant, the Nevada Energy Commission's plan to require solar technologies for all new housing developments will not be fulfilled. It will be a sad millennium for millions when the neon lights go out forever.

Are There Any More Perfect Phrases for Letters of Support?

Before you give your partners examples of perfect phrases to include in their letters of support or before you begin to formulate your own perfect phrases for letters of support, think forward. By this, I mean think about what you would want to read in a letter of support if you were a grant officer or a foundation director. What touches your heart? What makes one letter stand out over another? Be creative, be different, and, most importantly, don't be afraid to create your own perfect phrases.

About the Author

Dr. Beverly A. Browning has been consulting in the areas of grant writing, contract bid responses, and organizational development for over two decades. Her clients have included units of local and county municipal governments, state and federal government agencies, school districts and colleges, social and human service agencies, hospitals, service associations, and Fortune 500 corporations. Dr. Browning has assisted clients throughout the United States in receiving awards of more than $100 million.

She is the author of a dozen grants-related publications, including *Grant Writing for Dummies™* (2001 and 2005, Wiley), *Grant Writing for Educators* (2004, Solution Tree), *How to Become a Grant Writing Consultant* (2001 and 2005, BBA, Inc.), *Faith-Based Grants: Aligning Your Church to Receive Abundance* (2005, BBA, Inc.), and *Winning Strategies for Developing Grant Proposals* (2006, Thompson).

She holds degrees in Organizational Development, Public Administration, and Business Administration. Dr. Browning is a grant writing course developer and online facilitator for Education To Go, faculty member at the U.S. Chamber of Commerce Institute for Organization Management and Rio Salado College Online, and a member of the Advisory Board for the University of Central Arkansas Community Development Institute. She is also a member of and chapter resource developer for the American Association of Grant Professionals.

Visit her Web site at **www.grantsconsulting.com**.